With best wishes

Christopher Booker

# RECOLLECTIONS OF A SOUTHWOLD GP

---

## DR CHRISTOPHER HOPKINS

Published in the United Kingdom by Dr Christopher Hopkins.
© Dr Christopher Hopkins, 2020

First published in September 2020.
ISBN 978-1-913532-21-5

Design and artwork by Harcourt Communications, Harringworth,
Northamptonshire NN17 3AH.

Printed and bound by CPI Group (UK) Ltd, Croydon CR0 4YY.

For my family, friends and patients,
and in memory of my dear wife Mary

## Acknowledgements

I am very grateful to my family and friends
who urged me when I recounted stories of my life to write this book.

To Dr James Le Fanu for the foreword
and to Bruce Kent for his account on the cover.

To Jo Charles for typing my original scrawl.

To Pernickety Kate for the first editing.

To my son-in-law Lindsay Clubb for all his time in setting out the photos.

To Jamie James for getting up with his drone at five in the morning
to take photos of Southwold on the cover.

To Richard Nixon and George Edgeller for the final production.

Last but not least to my beautiful wife Mary
for not once grumbling at the time it took writing in the last year of her life.

# Contents

# Foreword

Christopher Hopkins's memoir – encompassing more than 30 years as a family doctor in Southwold on the Suffolk coast – is full of interest. His might seem an idyllic life. When he first arrived in the 1950's, he tells us, the local fishermen still sold the day's catch of herring on the beach, while out to sea porpoises could be seen frolicking and a Thames barge in full sail plied its way to and from Great Yarmouth. But General Practice in those days was arduous and demanding with a heavy workload of twice daily surgeries, home visits while also being on call at night and at weekends. When not delivering babies at home he might be administering an anaesthetic, interpreting X-rays, supervising his patients in his local cottage hospital or suturing wounds in its small operating theatre. So arduous certainly but also immensely varied and fulfilling not just professionally but personally fostered by bonds of friendship, trust and respect established over many years.

Dr Hopkins' memoir extends beyond an entertaining and insightful account of a life well lived serving the citizens of Southwold. 'History', observed the writer G. K. Chesterton 'is a high point of advantage from which alone you can see the world in which we live'. And from the high point of advantage of looking back over the last several decades his experience illuminates two historical events of great importance.

First his career coincided with what now seems like a Golden Age of medical discovery and innovation. It is difficult to imagine what life must have been like as a medical student back in 1945 when deaths in childhood from polio and diphtheria were still a commonplace and there were few effective treatments for most of the illnesses a doctor encountered. By the time he retired 45 years later he had lived through an epoch of unprecedented medical achievement where the previously inconceivable – open heart surgery, transplanting kidneys, test tube babies – had become routine.

Next Dr Hopkins career also coincided with the founding of that most beneficent of social experiments the National Health Service. This permitted, as Dr Hopkins observes, doctors 'to practice as we thought best, to look after patients without fear of the cost and to prescribe what I wished and to refer patients to hospital as I liked'.

These then were intensely optimistic times. Then gradually and for several reasons the precious freedom to respond appropriately to his patients' needs would be eroded by managerial interference. Dr Hopkins decision to retire early rather than submit to the immensely damaging Health Service 'reforms' imposed by the Conservative Government 1990 marks a watershed as increasingly doctors would be obliged to practice 'medicine by numbers' their income dependent on ticking boxes and following protocols.

Dr Hopkins singular achievement then is not just to convey in rich detail a significant chapter of the social history of Britain in the decades following the War but to affirm the virtues and values of good 'old fashioned' family doctoring.

**Dr James Le Fanu**

# Introduction

Many of us have an ambition throughout our lives of writing a book. I certainly had. It is only now to be fulfilled in time at the eve of my life. A book by Ronald Binns on George Orwell's connection with Southwold gave me a feeling of kinship. He was at Southwold when he had difficulty in getting his first book *Down and Out in Paris and London* published. I am not expecting to follow any further in his footsteps, but I have at least one other episode in common: dishwashing as a student at the Savoy Hotel, London.

As will be seen, chance came my way at many times in my life, whether it was to meet up with royalty, our Prime Minister, our most famous actor, or be the first in this country to use steroids or oral hypoglycaemics. It was to come again so many times in my personal life. But a main theme of the book is to compare General Practice in the mid to late 20th century with the present 21st century. In my time, GPs for the most part, were keen, fulfilled, happy and proud to be one of their profession. This was despite being on call 24/7 and at one time without any financial support for their premises or staff. The work was rewarding, and not so much in the financial sense. It was the satisfaction of being the true family doctor. Now, with very much higher incomes, GPs appear discontented and talk of stopping home visits, reducing themselves to a three-day working week (on call at night and weekends having long been relinquished).

It is my hope that my portrayal of a practitioner in my time at a small seaside town in rural Suffolk shows how working hard and playing hard can lead to a very happy and fulfilled life.

# PART ONE
# GROWING UP

# Childhood

I was born in 1927, in the interval between the two world wars. I was delivered by forceps, something I was going to learn to use myself later in life. My mother told me this in my forties, my instant reaction being to hold my head. At the time my parents were living at 103 Erskine Hill, Hampstead Garden Suburb, London, my mother having been installed there, along with her parents and siblings, by her brother in law Hugh Fairfax Cholmeley. My grandparents had been employed by Hugh as housekeeper and gardener at his home, Brandsby Hall in Yorkshire. However, after marrying their eldest daughter Alice, he felt it was not right to have them living there any more. He had declared his intention to marry her at the time of her birth in the household eighteen years previously. Hugh inherited and temporarily owned Gilling Castle nearby. This was eventually the reason that I came to school there, after it was acquired as a Preparatory School for Ampleforth College.

Hugh paid for my mother to be educated, boarding at the Notre Dame Convent at Clapham (my older sister Anne followed years later). Hugh also enabled my mother to go to the Royal Academy of Music. As a result she performed, giving musical accompaniment to silent movies of that time.

My mother's parents died not long after coming to London and her brother Charles left to marry. This now left my mother and her sister Hilda living in Erskine Hill on their own, and when my parents married, my father joined them. Hilda never married, one of the many women whose would-be husbands were killed in the slaughter of World War One. She continued to live with us for most of the rest of her life and became a second mother to me. I always liked her story of her nearly falling out of an upstairs window at Erskine Hill in her excitement at seeing a German Zeppelin coming down in flames.

# Egypt

My fourth birthday came on board a P&O liner on its way to Egypt. My father, a civil servant in the Exchequer and Audit department, was now attached to the military services in the Middle East with his head office at Kasr El Nil Barracks in the centre of Cairo. Britain had, at the time between the wars, the Protectorates of Egypt, Sudan, Palestine and Iraq. With one battalion of troops at Cairo, an Air Force squadron in the desert outside, another on the Suez Canal, a naval detachment at Alexandria, another battalion of troops at Jerusalem and a further two Air Force squadrons in Iraq, this is how we kept the peace in the Middle East in the first half of the 20th Century. How different the situation in the Middle East has been since.

How the two squadrons in Iraq managed to control the whole country was quite simple. If there was trouble somewhere, they dropped leaflets one day, warning the population they would drop bombs if they didn't behave the next.

My father, as part of his job, had to visit all these bases from Cairo once a year to supervise their accounts, the plane taking him the first part of his journey to Jerusalem being guided by a furrow in the Sinai desert sand. Our father amused my sister Anne and me with two stories of encounters at the Air Force Base outside Baghdad. Once, while sitting on the *thunderbox*, as it was called, in the small outside cabin loo, a huge snake coiled itself down in front of him from the roof. Edging himself out round the beast was quite tricky. Another story concerned a mongoose kept as a pet by the Squadron Leader in the room next door. The two rooms were connected by an open drain and my father had the alarming experience of waking in the night with the animal snuggling on his chest.

Another episode he liked to relate was his encounter on one of the airfields in Iraq with the aviator Jim Mollison. It was the early days of aviation with the pioneer flyers challenging each other. Mollison was on his way like Amy Johnson to make the fastest time from Britain to Australia. Needing several fuel stops, coming down in Iraq from Europe, he took off his outer pair of trousers (having needed the extra warmth in an open cockpit) and handed them to my father. My father wore them for a long time afterwards when gardening, referring to them as Mollison's bags.

My father had gone on ahead of us not knowing if Egypt was a suitable country for an English family to live in. He soon found many families already there and sent for us. Coming on board on our arrival at Port Said he found alone in the dining room his four-year-old son surrounded by a host of waiters, saying, with the menu in front of him, "I'll have sausage."

To grow up in the years 1931 to 1936 in Cairo in fact was idyllic. The British certainly felt they were the top dogs then. It made you so proud to see red all over the map of the world. I joined my elder sister Anne within a year, at a French school run by a Madame Morain with an English subsection. Assemblies were in French and I am told I did speak French, something that must have helped me to speak it later in life.

In all these years I can't remember the climate being unpleasant except on two occasions. There was only one day that I remember feeling exceedingly hot and being told the temperature was well over a hundred degrees Fahrenheit. The other time was the Khamaseen, a dry hot dusty wind, that blew off the desert once a year for a week or two. It made me very irritable. The family used to teasingly call it Christopher's Khamaseen temper. Photos at that time showed me wearing large hats with wide brims. It was believed then that you had to keep a cool head against the danger of sunstroke in the tropical sun. Hence the use of pith helmets. There was not the same fear of skin cancer. It was all discarded by the Desert Rats, the soldiers fighting in the North African desert in World War 2.

The great place to spend a large part of our time was at the Gezira Sporting Club on the island of Gezira in the middle of Cairo where most of the Europeans lived. The club was only for Europeans. With a manned gate and a surrounding high fence, it felt very safe. Inside apart from our large children's playground were a cricket field, polo field, a racecourse surrounding a golf course, a swimming pool, numerous tennis courts and a restaurant area. In the heyday of the Empire, wherever the British set themselves up in the world, they always made sure of being able to enjoy their sport.

We spent a large part of our time in the outdoor swimming pool open all the year round. Initially using gourds as water-wings, I soon learned to swim. Rather ambitions at first, I jumped in, only to start sinking to the bottom. My mother had to jump in after me fully clothed to rescue me. Daring to use higher and higher diving boards was always the greatest of fun. With a crowd of children, I can't remember much supervision.

We did have nannies. Our first, an Italian, Anne and I hated. We called her Piggy Nanny. Next came a sweet English girl, Helen. She left us to marry a sergeant in the Cairo garrison, but not before taking us to several children's parties at their mess. It was with Helen that I am sure I could have lost my life. She took us on an expedition to the Mouski, a warren of little shops in the centre of Cairo. There we were supposed to meet up with Helen's boyfriend to take us back by car, but we missed him. On our way back over Boulak Bridge to Gezira by bus, there was his open car lying on its side in the middle of the bridge. With no seat belts I would surely have been thrown out and killed.

In our final year, before our departure in April 1936, we had a 19-year-old German girl, whom we called Fräulein. We never knew her Christian name. She was blonde and freckled and I as a seven to eight-year-old quite fell for her. We had to converse in French as she did not speak English. This is perhaps the reason some of my French friends accuse me of speaking French with a German accent. Fraulein made me believe Germany had really won the war. When she took us to the German Embassy Christmas parties, I was more impressed by the grey uniformed warlike German toy lead soldiers than my own toy soldiers wearing busbies and red jackets. I became a proper little Nazi. But at the same time I was immensely proud of my country. I felt this at the celebrations of King George V's Jubilee watching the guns firing a salute on the Gezira Club golf course. When Madame Morain announced one morning at the school assembly that King George had just died, I was in tears.

On one occasion Fräulein had to travel to Alexandria to board a German warship there to sign up her allegiance to the Führer. I was smitten enough when back in England at our house in Rochester, that if I saw a blonde head passing along the top of our front hedge to run out calling Fräulein.

With nannies you only really met up with your parents on Sundays, the nanny's day off. But with the freedom allowed for children in bygone days, once at the Gezira Sporting Club we soon left the nannies chatting together in the playground while we were off to explore the vast area of the club. So started my adventurous spirit. In the latter part of my time with other English boys we formed gangs and had a sort of warfare against all the rest, the French and Italians. We never actually clashed.

The Irish Guards arriving in our last year to take over at Kasr El Nil Barracks brought with them a Catholic padre. This meant we could now attend Sunday Mass at the chapel in the barracks with the relief from long sermons in Italian at our local church on Gezira Island. It was my great joy to be able to sing hymns in English and in particular join the soldiers singing loudly *The Faith of our Fathers*.

In the same year, Anne and I were enlightened in our Faith by weekly classes at our school on a Saturday morning by an Italian priest. He talked of the bad English Protestants. He must have had a good effect on me, as I started to say my prayers with great fervour. One morning as I was kneeling at my bed my father entered the room and standing over me got very irritated when I didn't stop. At that time he himself had no particular religious allegiance.

In our time out there, we were to have an assortment of summer holidays. Our first was to the seaside resort on the Mediterranean at Aboukir, the scene of Nelson's defeat of the French. This was marked by my developing dysentery. It was blamed on the bad hygiene of our hotel. I was quite ill for several days, the feeling starting as I was sitting on the horse that took us to and from the beach, then taking me back to our hotel. I can still picture the white walls of my bedroom as I came round from my delirium.

The next summer we went back on leave to England. With the voyage taking two weeks each way, my father made it shorter by starting after us, travelling by boat to Naples and then taking the train back overland. 1933 was one of the best summers at home on record. My father bought an old jalopy. It was quite large with an upright windscreen. The registration number being ML he called it Margaret Lucy after his sister. So, being motorised, we were able to tour the country first visiting all the Hopkins family in Leicestershire. My grandfather had retired from his farm and was living in Leicester, but some cousins of my father were still farming for us to enjoy the harvest time. It was crossing a river on a ferry, being a very hot day, when I jumped in half-way across. It horrified all the passengers as they all thought a five-year-old was bound to drown.

We had started off the holiday with my mother's relations, the Moverleys at Hampstead Garden Suburb. It still being term time for our two cousins Carol and Clare, Anne and I to our disgust were made to join them at their Finchley convent. We felt it a bit unfair going back to school in our holidays, French schools having longer summer vacations. However, all in all, it was a very blissful time.

The journey back by boat to Egypt took the usual two weeks with the same ports of call en route. Although its ultimate destination was India and Australia, the liner was in no hurry, stopping off each time for one to two days. On the first stop at Gibraltar, I was always fascinated by the Barbary apes on the Rock. The ship then crossed the Straits to make a brief call at Tangiers and then all the way to Marseille. Again I enjoyed the climb up, this time by the funicular railway to look down on the port. Naples, the next stop, gave us plenty of time to visit Pompeii. But I remember being frightened whether we would get back to the ship in time. We did see one man arrive at the quayside as we had just cast off, shouting madly to let him on. As the gap widened, he jumped into a rowing boat to try and catch up, but we were gathering speed. I always felt so sorry for him.

Next stop, the last before Port Said, was Malta. There the story of goats wandering the streets just living off newspapers and other rubbish always intrigued me. Arriving at Port Said the ship as usual moored off shore. Waiting to land we were always greatly entertained by the Gully Gully man who came on board wearing his red hat tarboosh and flowing robes. He was so called as this was the sound he made while doing his tricks. We would make a circle round him while he extracted eggs, live chicks or other objects out of people's ears or pockets. At the same time young boys swam alongside the ship for coins to be thrown into the sea for them to dive for.

Having brought back on board with us Margaret Lucy, we set off in her from Port Said to Cairo. Halfway through the Delta there was a big bang, a part of the engine shot out through the bonnet and we came to a grinding halt. My mother, Anne and I got a lift onwards while my father waited for the local garage to find some part from another old engine and fit the car up.

Margaret Lucy was to take us on some marvellous jaunts into the desert. One such was with one or two other families to go and sleep out there for the night. Set up in a wadi, Anne and I slept on our camp beds under the brilliant stars. We were intrigued seeing the little jerboas hopping past us on the sand. At one time in the night we woke up to see a line of camels passing silently by in the moonlight. I was to make Anne laugh years later when visiting her in her nursing home with advanced Parkinson's disease. I reminded her about us sitting side by side on two loo seats, neatly carved out of a low rocky ledge to do our duty and she saying, "Have I done enough?"

The next summer we went to stay at Lake Timsah on the Suez Canal. It was there that aged six with my father and sister I swam across the canal and back, pushing the inner tube of a tyre in front of us. In that way I can boast to have swum at that age from Africa to Asia and back.

Taking us out on the lake in a dinghy in a high wind, by it seemed a very inexperienced young walad, we gybed and nearly capsized. My father in a high state of anxiety swore at the poor boy. The sand yacht we went on in the desert at an RAF base nearby was more relaxing, whizzing along on terra firma. It was all quite different from the sails we had in the stately feluccas on the Nile at Cairo.

In 1935 we took the boat from Port Said to Cyprus. In April I had had a younger sister, Rosemary. Seeing her a day or two after she was born in the American Hospital on Gezira Island, I expected to see a baby sitting up who I could play ball with. I was quite put out to see just a squiggly little thing in a cot.

Cyprus was another blissful time. For the first part, we were up in the cool of the mountains at Mount Troodos. There was no hotel there. The

Cypriot owner had laid out on the mountainside a series of marquees with iron bedsteads and normal household furniture inside. Anne and I slept inside one with Fräulein. It was such a change from hot dry dusty Cairo to have walks through the cool of the pine trees and down valleys with rushing streams. At one spot a spring gushed from the ground and the stream then soon formed pools to bathe in.

My father took a party of us children and another mother on a long walk down a stream from Mount Troodos. We became lost not finding a path crossing the stream to take us back to the camp. At our picnic stop downstream I wandered away from the others to come across the mother like Aphrodite arising from the waves standing naked in a pool. I was amazed at the whiteness of her skin. To find our way back upstream the same way we came down, was confusing with other streams joining in all directions. It was getting dark. My father being responsible for so many children must have been very worried. With great relief we found the tower marking the top of Mount Troodos from where we knew the path back to our camp.

Two events were organised at the camp for children which caused great excitement. The first was to gather pine cones in sacks for a giant bonfire. Being paid for this, it was the first time I had ever actually held any money. The second was a competition for best model village made out of pine cones and other objects lying around.

At that time in 1935, Italy was invading Abyssinia (now known as Ethiopia). There was actual talk of the possibility of going to war. It amused my father that at this time of crisis the one small garrison was stationed nearby at their summer quarters on Mount Troodos. What were they doing? Just playing cricket against himself and other visitors. There was in front of the church at the army camp a board that read Church of England. Puzzled, with my patriotic spirit I asked my mother why couldn't we attend there then?

We finished the holiday staying at the one small hotel on the shore at Famagusta, owned by the proprietor of the holiday camp on Mount Troodos. A young Greek Cypriot lad named Demetrius took Anne and me sailing in his small dinghy up the coast to some pomegranate groves.

I will always remember him saying, "If there's a war, I will fight for the British Empire," feelings quite different post-war with EOKA (the nationalist guerrilla organisation that fought a campaign for the end of British rule in Cyprus).

The boat came alongside the quay in the dark at Famagusta to take us back to Port Said. On the voyage we encountered a great storm that made us all very sick and my mother very cross with Fräulein for looking after herself and neglecting Rosemary. At first, the train taking us back to Cairo from Port Said went along the Suez Canal. There passing down it alongside us was an Italian warship obviously on its way to Abyssinia, with Italian troops up all the rigging waving and cheering madly. Fräulein horrified Anne and me with tales of the Abyssinians creeping up to the Italians in the night with scissors to cut off their willies. I can't remember what term she used in French or perhaps in German. Fraulein was also to frighten Anne and me on another occasion when we came across a young Egyptian man in the street with a disfigured face, his nose completely eroded away. In its place were two cavities. She said if we picked our noses the same would happen to us. No doubt it was leprosy.

On our return we moved to the top floor of the newly built Zamalek block of flats that gave us marvellous views over Cairo to the Mokattam hills. At night the moon shone especially brilliantly in the clear sky. My mother's upright piano had to be taken up the six flights of stairs. A gang arrived to do the heaving with a man in charge whose sole job it seemed was just to do the grunting for them. We had to pay him the most. In the flat we kept the usual staff – a cook and a manservant. In our last months the latter was a tall Sudanese with fine chiselled black features so different from the sallow Egyptians. I always liked the sight of my mother every morning sitting at her desk in the hall, the cook standing beside her taking the shopping order and duties for the day. In our previous flat my mother had a great shock going into the kitchen two weeks before Christmas and seeing a turkey strutting around. Asking the cook what it was all about, he answered, "Turkeys are so much cheaper bought early at the market."

My father, after working in the morning, played tennis at the Gezira Club every afternoon the year round, so became quite a good player. He was made the tennis chairman. I felt very proud of him as he made the announcements over the loudspeaker at the many tennis tournaments. Helen Moody, seven times champion at Wimbledon, called at Cairo on her way back from Australia to give an exhibition match. After asking my father to give her a knock up, they decided to play a set. To his astonishment my father won, such was the difference between the best lady player in the world and a good male club player. My father was far too busy to give me a game. My opportunity came by seizing one of the Egyptian ball boys. We had a great game, probably my first ever, with him using a piece of board shaped into a racquet. At the end he asked for baksheesh (money). I never carried any. Feeling in his debt I asked my father for a piaster (a small unit of money). A day or so later with the ball boys all lined up for a tournament I went up to the one I thought was him and handed over the money. It was probably to the astonishment of a quite different walad (boy).

One most exciting excursion we made several times was in a large party. It often happened when the children boarding back in England returned once in the year for their summer holidays. We all took a camel or a donkey from the long line at the foot of the escarpment, the Sphinx and the Great Pyramid towering above. We then rode along the edge between the desert and the delta plain to picnic further along. At one spot there were several small pyramids. I tried a camel at first but didn't like the way they lurched, nearly throwing you off when they got up, going forward one way then the other. Perched high up they seemed to amble along so slowly. Much more exciting were the donkeys; they knew, when on the way back, that they were going for their feed. When your walad wasn't looking, you gave your donkey a kick. They immediately went off at a fast trot, with the walads shouting as they tried to catch up.

Another excitement was the RAF open day at their airbase in the desert outside Cairo, at Heliopolis. There I had the special thrill in those early days of aviation to have a short flight in a small single engine plane. In the middle of the display a dramatic announcement was made that the Imperial Airways mail plane from London was due to arrive on its way to India and Australia or possibly down to the South African Cape. The air route to the Cape had been opened up just ten years before. It duly landed. Close up the plane looked huge, parked with the fuselage at an angle into the air. Climbing inside one felt one was seeing the beginning of a new era.

A last adventure for my father, Anne and myself was to go inside and then climb the Great Pyramid. It was so odd that tourists coming to Cairo did this in the week they were there, while we left it to the last week before our departure. A small entrance on one side led you by a short passage to a long staircase, taking you up to the chamber at the very heart of the pyramid. There you could stare at the empty sarcophagus and wonder about its occupant. It was all lit by electricity. We were told, to make us feel chilled, that previously visitors went in with a guide holding a candle. At one point they would blow it out and demand baksheesh. (I still remember a few Arabic words: 'imshi walad' – *go away, boy* and 'cobya moiya' – *glass of water*.)

After exploring the inside of the Great Pyramid, we went outside to immediately climb to the top. It is no longer allowed. I had the privilege at eight years old. I was so annoyed that the Arab guide who took us would insist on holding my hand, a boy, and not my sister, a girl. I can't remember the blocks of stone being all that huge or difficult to climb. It felt very good at the top. I was always very intrigued by watching several mad Englishmen having a race to be the fastest to the top and down again.

Years later I had the chance of getting back my feeling for the Great Pyramid with the help of a lady patient of mine well into her seventies. She was taking a day trip to Cairo to visit the pyramid when it was possible on Concorde. I asked her to bring back a stone from near its base which she did.

In the last six months I was to make the great achievement at Madame Morain's of being moved up to my elder sister's class. I felt so proud to be with her and her friends. It was then that I wrote a long essay on Clive of India that I kept for years. Sadly it has recently gone missing. Was this a portent of me being the writer manqué?

It was time for us to take our final trip in a P&O liner, the *Moultan*, back to England. As to be related later, I was to see the *Moultan* again in 1951 while on passage in a yacht to Gibraltar. Fräulein came with us to go on to visit her parents in Berlin. My parents said she cried when they saw her off at Tilbury. She said it was not for them but for Christopher. She went back to Egypt before war broke out. We were told after the war by a friend who stayed there, that she married an Italian, a Signor Bruno, only for them to be both interned when Italy entered the war. Staying in Berlin in the early part of this millennium, I reckoned Fräulein, if she had returned to Berlin, could still be alive in her 80s. Trying the few Brunos in the telephone directory, sadly I got no reply.

## Rochester

It was now 1936. My father, rather than return to London, to be away from the big city opted for a lesser post attached to the naval dockyard at Chatham. He fell on his feet, as at hand was the Officers' tennis club, at which he soon became its captain and enjoyed a lot of inter-club tennis. In his last year he won the Kent Club Championship.

I was back in an English school at the King's School Rochester, and was to be nicknamed the Egyptian Cat. I found my level of reading and writing from my French school to be much higher than my peers, while at swimming there was only one other swimmer of my age to compete with me on sports day.

My religion made a difference as I was soon to find out. At first unknown to my mother and my second mother Aunt Hilda, I was not only attending scripture lessons and morning prayers at a C of E school but also attended services at Rochester Cathedral. They were horrified when they found out as any participation at that time for a Catholic at non-Catholic prayers was forbidden. For morning prayers and scripture lessons, I then had to stay outside the classroom. I found it difficult to understand the difference when I heard the Creed being said with the words "I believe in the Catholic Church." Unlike Bishop Fisher of Rochester at the Reformation, I was not to be then an early martyr when I denied my faith. This happened with a so-called friend in an isolated spot on the banks of the Medway, when we were confronted by two much larger boys. My friend, to divert an expected assault away from himself, pointed to me saying, "He's a Roman Catholic." To my eternal shame, like Peter, I fiercely denied it. But it was really more out of anger than fear at being betrayed in this way by a friend.

My adventurous spirit that started at the Gezira Sports Club was soon able to be unleashed again. Even at eight years old, parents (and mine in particular at that time) were quite happy to allow their young to go out roaming on their own. I bought an air gun to go potting at sparrows, quite numerous then. But the discovery of the old Napoleonic fortifications in a park by the river Medway was the means of much exciting exploration. Entering through a hole in a wall led to underground passages leading to dusty rooms, one filled with old uniforms and on to further passages. No one else apart from my close friends seemed to have found them. We went by candlelight at first but then saved our pocket money for a torch. I was to discover further old fortifications to explore on my own at the Chatham Tennis Club. The hillsides of Chatham and Rochester seemed riddled with them, and only us to enjoy them.

In one passage the roof had fallen in, leaving just a small space to crawl through. It was leading on down to the river for perhaps even more exciting things to find. We thought better of it which was just as well. Doing our explorations in secret, if anything had happened, we would have just vanished.

The period between the wars was a good time to be lucky enough to be middle class. We had the means, with decent houses and help at home with maids. (It was a term used for domestics then.) Even my father on a modest income could afford a maid at seventeen shillings (80p) five and a half days a week, with hours 9-5.30pm. Having a car meant you could get about to enjoy yourself. School leaving age was fourteen, which meant starting work then and therefore not so many teenagers about in the holiday times. The middle class had the place to themselves as best depicted in the much loved adventures of 'Swallows and Amazons'. Mostly I think they were respected for being 'educated' by those who weren't, not so much for being richer. An educated man with some reservations about accent was known as 'a gentleman'. I had a taste of this myself as an eleven-year old, when staying at my cousin's farm in Yorkshire. The farm workers called me 'Master Christopher'. I rather liked it. This all smacks of class distinction but it was a fact, and I was certainly aware of it. It was the raising of the school leaving age and chance of university education for all now that has made the difference.

When my parents were out for the evening, sitting with our maid Kathleen and a friend, baby-sitting, I had the chance to read their magazines, one in particular 'The Star'. They obviously felt guilty about this as they asked me to promise not to tell my parents. I was puzzled. There was a lot about boy meets girl. Then she felt faint and found she was pregnant. How come? I was to find out when for two holidays, a brother and sister of my age, Prinia and David, came to stay as their parents were in Africa. They explained to me the facts of life. I couldn't believe babies came into the world that way. Prinia had to demonstrate. It was my first gynaecological lesson. It was all very innocent really.

In my early years in the thirties people talked of 'the War'. It had been the war to end all wars. But by 1938 I became aware of the fear of another. There was a temporary relief in September after the Munich Agreement to make us feel the blissful days of peace could continue. But being issued with gas masks that Autumn made the risk more real. We were given the chance of trying them out by putting them on in a van in the city centre filled with tear gas. The operator invited you to take them off inside for a moment to realise how efficient they were.

We had several enjoyable holidays in those three years before war broke out again. The first in 1937 was to Suffolk staying at Church Farm, Dunwich. My father had bought a Morris Ten, with its thermometer on the bonnet, for us to cross over the Thames by the Tilbury ferry. We always walked to the beach at Minsmere through the woods, passing a monkey puzzle tree that fascinated me. Never forgotten, searching for it recently I found it hidden amongst other trees, grown much taller.

The farm loo arrangement also intrigued me. You walked across the farmyard to climb upstairs into a barn. There at the far end along a bench were three loo seats in a row of different sizes and heights, reminiscent of father, mother and baby bear. The result was collected in the farmyard below. It was harvest time and with my father and sister Anne we took our positions with sticks waiting for the rabbits to come out of the corn. One did run out near my father and with the good eye that he had, he killed it. I will always remember the look of horror on his face.

The annual pilgrimage to Dunwich in memory of the many churches now under the sea took place on one of the Sundays we were there. With Mass being said in a field just across the road from the farm, it saved us a long journey to church. Our farmer made the most of it by opening his farmyard as a car park. After Mass we processed down the village street to the cliff edge where prayers and a blessing over the sea were made. I also very much enjoyed a ride down the street on the back of one of the Suffolk Punches as they were taken at the end of their day's work to a field at the end on the left where now a car park exists. The Pilgrimages continued on first taking up my practice at Southwold and then ended. The gathering for Mass was changed to the grounds of the Old Priory near the edge of the cliff. On one year, for some reason, it took place on Southwold Common.

Summer 1938 saw one of the best holidays I have had. We stayed on a farm, Lethwyr, at Penycwm on the Pembrokeshire coast. Now with motorways people will be surprised to hear that it took us a day and a half from the other side of England to get there. Setting off in the early hours from Rochester, we breakfasted as we steered round London to the south. Reaching Wales in the evening, having passed through every town and village on the way, we camped in a field by a stream for the night to arrive at our destination next day. At the farm it was harvest time where I was to have much fun. Going with the farm workers I amused my parents when I related how they spoke in Welsh: "Blah blah blah ... bloody fool! Blah blah blah ... bloody fool!" They didn't seem to have that particular expression in Welsh. With ponies on the farm I rode every morning with my father and sister. Apart from the donkeys in Egypt, I hadn't ridden before. I am sure we were cantering on our first ride, though admittedly I was holding on to the saddle. It makes me wonder at the cautious start to riding that normally takes place. On one occasion we went down to the beach where surely the canter turned into a gallop.

Afternoons were spent on the beach. It was just a short walk down the valley. There were high cliffs and large stretches of sands. Walking across the wide beach to the edge of the sea I always felt the Atlantic rollers were higher than me. The daunting matter of getting in and out of the water was always a question of waiting for the calmer waves in between the more fearsome ones. Our wire-haired terrier Peter fell the fifty or more feet over the cliff edge chasing rabbits but came to no harm.

We lived off the land, food being cooked by the farmer's wife. We had lamb and rabbit cooked in every fashion possible and it was delicious. Most mornings I went around with the rabbiter in his pony and trap to pick up the overnight catch in the gin traps. We always ended with the hold of the trap piled high. There was a huge black bull lying in a pen. The farmer's young children liked to show off walking onto him and jumping up and down, then inviting us the visitors to do the same. Daringly we did. For a youngster it was an ideal holiday.

The following year, 1939, the gloom of an impending war became deeper and deeper. The school was taken to an attractive country house, Scotney Castle in Kent, where it was to be evacuated if war came. I was intrigued by the Priest's hole, a Catholic family having lived there during penal times. However I was to go elsewhere.

We had a final holiday on a farm in Cornwall towards the end of August, feeling the inevitable war was about to happen. We went on to make a trip up to Yorkshire to stay with my mother's elder sister Alice and the Cholmeleys when war was at last declared. I never returned to Rochester.

# Ampleforth College 1939-1945
## Gilling Castle

Staying in the neighbourhood as war broke out, I was to come to Ampleforth by chance. So for this I have to thank Adolf Hitler. As Fr (Posh) Paul was to tell me, towering above me in the big passage of the Upper School three years later, "We lost several boys at the beginning of the war, but we gained two, you and Ken Gray." (He was later to be the school doctor and married the sister of a school friend Bob Campbell, later to be mentioned.) We were at the home of my uncle Hugh and Aunt Alice Fairfax-Cholmeley, namely Swathgill near Brandsby. Hugh had started life at Brandsby Hall, his family ancestral home. He had not only inherited a large estate there, but also Gilling Castle and its estate from his father. He in his turn had inherited it from his father, married to Harriet the last of the Fairfaxes. That entailed adding Fairfax to the Cholmeley name. It was a relative, Lady Ann Fairfax, who built a house on the other side of the valley at Ampleforth for her chaplain; that was then relinquished for a community of Benedictine monks returning from their exile in France looking for an English home. It was there that they started a College for boys in 1802 that has continued since.

Hugh sold the Castle and estate for £50,000 in 1893. As mentioned earlier, the story goes that when my aunt Alice was born at Brandsby Hall to the housekeeper and her gardener husband, Hugh, then in his twenties, vowed he would marry the girl when she grew up. He was true to his word, and did so when she was 18. (My mother was also born there.) Hugh's ancestors, the Cholmeleys, were an old Catholic family, as also were my mother's, the Moverleys, both claiming to have kept their Catholic faith through the reformation. They had a chapel at the Hall served by a monk from Ampleforth, Fr Bede Turner. He later became the titular abbot of Westminster. I was to meet him later when he came to our house in Hampstead. I remember kneeling and kissing his ring as I said goodbye in Golders Green bus yard. I say all this, as when war was declared on 3rd September while we were still at Swathgill, we were left isolated. Rochester, our home, we felt would be bombed, and Hugh had always promised we could stay if war broke out. Having been a day boy at the King's School, which was now being evacuated into the country, to join a Catholic prep school situated just three miles down the road, seemed the obvious thing to do.

My mother and Aunt Alice went to visit Fr Paul Nevill (Headmaster of the Upper school) to enquire about school fees and my possible entrance. My father, on a modest Civil Servant's salary, was worried about the fees. But Fr Paul would have none of it, saying that the nephew of the old owner just had to come, and he would help if necessary. So late in September, having come with my school trunk a day or two before, conveyed by cart and horse driven by my cousin Richard's farm hand up the school drive, and afterwards picking up coal from Gilling station, I was sitting in the common room waiting for the other boys to arrive by train. I was aged 11, feeling very elated and excited, with a great deal of relief, not to be the 'Roman' outsider any longer.

I was certainly to enjoy my year at Gilling. In my first term my mother, still living with the Cholmeleys, walked the three miles every Sunday to Mass in our chapel. (Both Hugh and Alice had given up their faith.) Later Fr Jerome Lambert, an Ampleforth monk, then parish priest to Brandsby village, told me he had visited Hugh when he was dying a few months later in March 1940. He had offered to hear his confession, to get the retort, "Youth was always insolent." Fr Jerome was then in his early thirties. But he did manage to get him to agree to make an absolute contrition (a way of expressing regrets from love of God for any sins in your life ) when he left.

Hugh was buried in the Brandsby churchyard next to his old game-keeper. This village church fascinatingly had been rebuilt by Hugh's fore-bear on a new site further away from their Hall as he had felt the old one was too close. The village now has its unique church in the Italian style with a flattish roof, such was the power of even a Catholic squire. I was able to meet and have a good chat with my Mum after Mass sitting by the fire in the great entrance hall, a picture of Lady Ann Fairfax looking down on us. Fr Henry would often join us with a greeting of "Hello, mother Hopkins." I loved the daily Mass and was especially thrilled when I was able to join in by serving at the altar.

Although very happy, I was to have a series of boils on a knee, which interfered with rugger. This was played on a field in the valley, shared with the farmer's cart horses. A shovel was kept on the side to remove the middens before play; no fear of tetanus in those days.

For the Christmas holidays we were back at Swathgill. Nothing much had happened in the so-called phoney war. The main difference in the country was the rationing of petrol. My father, still left behind at Rochester, saved up his ration in bottles, only to find some had burst in the frost. He managed to join us in Yorkshire but then sadly had to sell the Morris Ten for £20 at an Easingwold garage. (I was able to read in my grandmother Moverley's marriage certificate that her father had been a blacksmith at

Easingwold, perhaps a forebear of the present day garage owner.) Another sadness was saying goodbye to my pet dog, a wire-haired terrier called Peter, my faithful companion on all my boyish escapades. He had to be farmed out to a lovely couple, the Whites, as we now had no home. But I was still able to visit Peter later, on whole holidays at the Upper School, when they would give me and my friend Hardy great feasts.

Around the New Year the snow began to fall and the weather freeze. It was to be the longest wintry spell until two years after the war in 1947. Pictures came back of the British Expeditionary Force and the French in the snow on the Maginot Line in France. We were feeling sorry for the Finns fighting in the snow against the Russians.

On New Year's Eve my elder sister Anne went to a dance with our cousins and came back with the news that not only had she met an Ampleforth boy, the school doctor's son Vidal, but that the Gilling lakes were frozen and people including the monks were skating on them. The monks were playing ice hockey.

The next day Anne and I with our one bicycle set out to join them. It was all great fun. One excitement was Fr Jerome daringly driving his old jalopy over the ice. He was an absolute character, completely mad, but wonderful fun. He was later to be my lawless Sea Scout master. It was in the open dicky at the back of the car that Anne and I sat with mother in front, when Fr Jerome picked us up at the end of the drive to take us to his Sunday Mass at Brandsby. He was the serving chaplain there. On the first occasion, after it had frozen really hard that night, he arrived grinning all over. The hill up the road had been too icy, but somehow by turning the car round and reversing in the adjoining field, he had managed it. He amused my mother on another occasion when after the car came to a grinding halt, Fr Jerome jumped out, opened the bonnet, took a twig from the hedge, put it in the engine, and was ready to go again. I later went back to the Gilling lakes to find them deserted and a thaw setting in. The ice creaked ominously as I walked over it. Determined to explore further I went on to discover the Yearsley reservoir nearby. This was even more isolated. I couldn't resist trying the ice, again with the same weird creaking noise. I was lucky to escape alive.

The Easter term began with more snow falling. My return was tinged with sadness because my mother was to come for the first Sunday Mass only, as she was then parting for London to live with her brother's family, the Moverleys. Our time at Swathgill was up. The snow kept coming. It always seemed to be falling as I looked out from my classroom window. I wanted it to go on and on, as we had such fun tobogganing on a steep hill by Gilling Castle, now part of the school golf course. Eventually by mid-term the thaw came and with it, fog. I remember one particular walk in soggy snow with visibility down to a few yards.

Isolated as we were in the Yorkshire countryside the war passed us by. In the first months when an air raid warning was given somewhere in the county we were ushered into the cellars, but this was soon given up. But a letter home when in the Upper School does describe a dog fight overhead in the air happening then.

Good memories remain of toast and dripping in the basement corridor at elevenses, also of being read to by the headmaster Fr Maurus, a very genial person, in his room after supper to ten or so of us. More episodes of a story, keeping us on tenterhooks, followed every night. Fr Henry, another genial and happy person, would get us excited and interested, making little figures out of acorns and fir cones. Holy Week came during the term. I remember in particular praying at the altar of repose, and fervently saying I wanted to be a priest. It was something I was to fight against during the rest of my school days, not an uncommon feeling shared with other of my school friends – we felt a conflict between our calling and the things we might miss out on in life. Everything about the Mass and services in our little timber roofed chapel was wonderful. I can say without a doubt my year at Gilling was the holiest in my life. I wonder if I committed even one venial sin. And so another term ended.

The Easter holidays were spent in London with the Moverleys. I was able to compare notes with my sister Anne, boarding in a convent school. (The Notre Dame Clapham had been closed for fear of air raids and girls transferred to the sister convent at Teignmouth. Funnily enough, whereas London remained unscathed until September, in the first year of the war Teignmouth, as my sister told me in her letters, had tip and run raids through that summer.) Her experiences were so different from mine. They were never allowed out of the sight of nuns at any time.

The return for the summer term was postponed at least once as there was no place for the school train from London. We had carriages for over 100 boys to York, and then a special train laid on for the many meeting there to Gilling. The reason for the delay was priority for troop movements. At this time my father had volunteered to join the Army, for some administrative post behind the lines with the British Expeditionary Forces in France. His reason, I am sure, was that it was better paid than his civilian job, so he could better afford the 40 guineas a term at Ampleforth and those for my sister. He had already served in the last year of World War 1 in the Royal Engineers. (He often joked that from the moment he landed in France in August 1918 the Germans started to retreat. Firing mortar gas shells in the same part of the line where Adolf Hitler was gassed and invalided out, my father said if only he had done his job properly maybe World War II could have been prevented.) This time round, my father was only just able to get out in time from Boulogne before the Germans broke through to the coast. His efforts to support his children's education had very nearly made him a prisoner of war for the duration.

Summer term was idyllic. The sun shone constantly. Out of the blue, on one of these days Fr Maurus would announce at breakfast that today would be a holiday. Matron would provide us with sausages, and we would go off to the lakes and cook them in the open. We would all cheer and flick our fingers in delight. On our cubbing days we did the same thing, making dens in the woods and bracken.

Games started with athletics. It was practising the high jump that I fell awkwardly and dislocated my right wrist. I was taken to the physics lab at the College over the valley, where Dr Vidal X-rayed it on some primitive machine. He then replaced the joint and plastered it. Dr Vidal had a reputation of having taken a soldier's appendix out in World War 1 with a tin opener. My injury resulted in my being unable to take part in the athletics or in the beginning of the cricket season, a bitter blow. It was while staying in the common room one afternoon, as the rest were on the playing fields, that I heard a news bulletin on the wireless that the

Germans had broken through on the Western Front and the allies were in retreat. The school authorities had kept it all quiet up till then. One piece of bad news we had heard previously was the German invasion of Rumania. Prince Ghyka of that country had been sent by his parents to England at the onset of war, whilst they stayed behind themselves. Some boys pitilessly teased him about this, which made him cry. He was beside me in the dormitory. I had no idea of a title then. Perhaps it came later, but in any case, titles meant nothing in the milieu of school life.

I wanted the summer term to just go on and on. I was so happy. I did manage to start playing cricket at about half term, at first in the 2nd XI and later in the 1st to replace Bob Campbell as wicket keeper. He had had to return home as his father was seriously ill. Towards the end of term, a croquet lawn was set up, which was great fun. The end of term exams came. I had been put in the second form with boys in fact younger than myself. I felt in Latin in particular I wasn't given enough to do, so copied bits of grammar that we weren't doing from a boy in the class above me. In this way when it came to the line-up for the total exam results, I came in the top five or so, much to the amazement of my form master. I won the Geography prize, but heard a master saying how low even the top marks had been in that subject.

I had been doing carpentry, and in the last week I was to do something that weighed on my conscience for half the summer holidays. I took a piece of sandpaper without asking. Afterwards I felt this was stealing, and could be a mortal sin. I lived with this until arriving in London in September to stay with my Moverley Aunt and Uncle, just in time for the Battle of Britain to reach there. Crouching in their air raid shelter under the kitchen floor, when the air raid siren had sounded, I was filled with fear. Then the glorious moment – I went on my roller skates to St Edward's, Golders Green (where I had been baptised and my parents married) to confession. Having cleared my conscience, the bombs, I then felt, could drop and I wouldn't care a fig. But this was to be the only anxiety in an otherwise gloriously happy year at Gilling Castle, from the first view of it at the end of that long drive on cousin Richard's horse and cart.

## Junior House 1940-41

My stay at Ampleforth College was to last the exact length of the war. The first year at Gilling passed blissfully, as already recounted. The next stage over the valley, first for one year at Junior House and then four years in the Upper School, was in many ways grimmer, until arriving in the sixth form in the last two years. Then, from sleeping in a bleak dormitory, and the use of a bare common room in the day, you had a room to share with just one other. Junior House at that time was in an even worse position than the Upper School. To help other schools threatened by bombing, Ampleforth had given over most of the Junior House building, first to the York Quaker School Bootham for a short time, then to the Catholic prep school Avisford, from the South Coast. This meant we only had the use of just two dormitories and the Chapel. Otherwise we had to walk to the far end of the main school building for a refectory and common room as well as classrooms. We had no feeling of a home. One little thing to brighten us up was seeing the Avisford's headmaster's pretty red-headed daughter, whom we nicknamed 'Tizer the appetiser'. But as time went by you were able to form firmer and firmer friendships, which certainly helped to tolerate the harder side of boarding school, the repetitive term after term of leaving family and home for a period of ten weeks, without in those days any break. I remember once returning on the train to school, in about my third year, with that sinking feeling in my stomach thinking this was going on for ever.

One bane that was to plague me through those five years, and to a diminishing extent, thereafter, was the fear of blushing. It had started quite suddenly in the days before beginning at Junior House. Sitting on the lawn having tea at the Moverleys in North London with my cousins Carol and Clare and sister Anne, the group of them started to laugh at me for some reason, said something in a teasing way, and then said, "You're blushing." Such is how phobias begin. In later life I was to help people with this fear with hypnotherapy. If only I had had this help then. One reason for feeling lack of confidence at that time was the instability in my life because of the effects of war. Having to leave our home in Rochester at the onset, we had no real home for the next four years.

Starting at Junior House, having done so well in Latin at the end of year exams at Gilling, I was put in the Classics class. We were supposed to be the brains. We started Greek which I loved. In our year we had the younger brother of the then novice Basil Hume (later Cardinal Archbishop of Wesminster) and a son of the Belgian Prime Minister Pierlot. The family had escaped from the German invasion. Two elder brothers were sadly burnt one year later on the school train from London with some 5-6 others, when boys playing with matches set it on fire. A group of us were to see the elder brother Basil emerging from the monastery with other novices, for us to call out, "there go the conchies." It couldn't have helped Basil's guilt, he was to mention later, at not joining up.

Games on most days and scouts once a week were as usual to be the enjoyable part of life, at any rate for those good at it. I was fortunate enough to be in both the rugger and cricket first teams. In the House was Michael Hardy, later to play rugby for England, then very mature in size, dwarfing the rest of us. For this reason, to be fair on us smaller ones, he was put at full back and me at fly half. I was able to tease him about this at his silver wedding anniversary at the Savoy years later. At athletics I was able to win the high jump against Pike, who had won it at Gilling the year before, when I had to call off with a dislocated wrist. Poor Pike being unpopular, I got all the encouraging cheers from the House. At scouts we used every week a tumbledown building, isolated in the middle of the valley, called Mole Catcher's Cottage. There we cooked delicious stews, all highly peppered, followed by exciting activities, war games etc in the valley around or over at the lakes.

For the last term in the summer I was made a House monitor. On the last night of the previous term Fr Peter Utley our housemaster, had called me into his room to tell me so. He made a big thing of encouraging me that I had leadership. He knew I was really shy, and this was to boost my confidence. I found it all rather embarrassing. Being watched constantly in this way by both Fr Peter and later Fr Terence, regarding one's development, made it always feel a strain. But as their names suggest they were only really being fatherly.

For a week after the end of the summer term the scouts were holding a camp over at the Gilling lakes. I didn't really want to go as I was dying to get back to the family, now renting rooms in a farmhouse near Warwick, where my father's office had been evacuated. It rained all week, which didn't help. I was a patrol leader, and the unfortunate unpopular Pike was transferred to me from another patrol, having tried to run away. I must have been regarded as kind. We did the overnight stay away together. And so ended my second year at Ampleforth.

### Upper School St Aidan's 1941-45

At the end of the summer term at Junior House we were asked to put down our chosen House in the Upper School. There was only one House that had a bad reputation. We all wanted to avoid it. It was St Aidan's. This was due to its Housemaster Fr Terence Wright being a strict disciplinarian and giving many beatings. It was a fact that that year's intake had been a bit of a rough crew, and perhaps worse for Fr T, they were no good at games. He himself had been Captain of rugger in the school and the last to beat our big rival Sedburgh in the twenties. He and Fr Peter were special friends – Fr Peter himself a great sportsman, having been a fast bowler for Hampshire before entering the monastery. They obviously arranged between them, in order to boost Aidan's prowess at sport, to send some of the best sporting boys of Junior House to him. So, like the others my first inkling of my destination was one week before term to find the dreaded yellow A for my trunk coming through the letter box. My mates were Michael Hardy, John Brodie, and Patrick McNulty from another prep school in Ramsgate. I will never forget that smile on Fr Terence's long red face, receiving us at the top of the stairs outside the common room. From then on, we knew it would be there at every new term. I am sure he regarded us as his boys, as a father would miss us after we had been away.

St Aidan's in those days was situated in the main building, with no entity of its own. The dormitory was in the attic. Fr Terence, or Tintax as we called him, really was as hard as nails, but as I was to realise as time went by, he had a real warmth underneath. He had a small sitting room on the first floor with easy chairs and often the wireless blaring. These were the only comfortable chairs we could use, but we didn't always want to be sitting with our housemaster in breaks. The common room consisted of desks against all the walls with hard benches to sit on. On one wall there hung a well-known reproduction of a Dutch painting. Equally well known to us was that written on its reverse were the names of all those who had had house beatings from the head monitors, and the number of strokes given.

There were some latrines communal to all the school at the top of the big passage around the corner. They were the only place apart from one's semi-cubicled bed where one could be alone. There were some communal baths that we used twice a week. For ordinary washing there was a sort of gallery with rows of basins that we shared with at least one other House. Against the wall running the length of the gallery was a low trough with taps. These were our only means of washing after games, whether it was rugger or anything else. Another building housed refectories for some four Houses. That was it. Classrooms and laboratories adjoined in separate buildings. Outside was a theatre, gym, indoor rifle range, a parade ground for PT (physical training) and for the OTC (Officers Training Corps) as the JTC (Junior Training Corps) was described in those days. Down the valley in front of the school and monastery were the playing fields, the cricket pitches, the main rugger pitch surrounded by the athletic track, and an outdoor swimming pool. In the further distance was the forest of rugger posts, so well described by Lawrence Dallaglio (later England's Rugby captain). Joining the school to the monastery was the Church, at that time half the old original building being for the school and on the other side of the large dividing altar, the new Gilbert Scott-designed part for the monks.

The day started (as at Gilling and Junior House) with Mass every day, except for a blissful extra half hour lie in on Thursdays, with an additional High Mass on Sundays, and then Vespers or Compline in the evening. I never heard anyone complain about this. In the main we were most devout. In the sixth form you were allowed to get up a bit earlier before the usual 7.15am to serve an individual monk's Mass in the crypt. Then in the interval before breakfast, to study, or in the summer you could have the great delight of rushing down to the outdoor pool. I found serving these individual Masses especially inspiring. One of the happiest times of my stay was in fact the three-day retreat we had one year at the end of Holy Week, finishing on Easter Sunday and then off for the holidays on the Monday. The happiness was no doubt enhanced by that end of term feeling, but I was completely absorbed in all the Holy Week ceremonies.

The harsher side of school soon became evident. In many ways those times were not far off Tom Brown's school days. One of the worst aspects was the lack of privacy, but then there were the official beatings of boys by boys. The head monitor of the house, after discussing it with the Housemaster, was allowed to beat a boy. Often this was for a very little offence. In my fourth term I was told at lunch time that I was to be beaten that night – the offence was that I had dared to ask permission from a more senior monitor, after being refused by a more junior one, to go down to the village at the time of a not very significant match. It showed bad house spirit. My accomplice was my pal Hardy, but he hadn't actually spoken so he was let off. Luckily, I was more in with Fr Terence, the head of the house not being a very sporty type, so managing to catch Fr T at teatime, I was also let off. But what a horrible wait. It was my turn later as a house monitor to witness beatings. It could go on for many strokes. I disliked it, but as it was all part of school life then, I accepted it. For deliberate infringements like smoking it was fair enough.

Life became rosier in the last two years, when in the sixth form you could share a room. It was with my great chum Michael Hardy. We had developed into bosom pals in our first year at St Aidan's. With Patrick McNulty we were a trio. Michael was to remain a good friend until his premature death at 66, and Patrick until he disappeared off to South Africa around 1951. Michael had a wicked sense of humour and had most of us in fits of laughter in his company. It could be at someone's expense, which wasn't exactly fair, but never against me. We both excelled at games, playing in the cricket and rugger first teams. I also represented the school at swimming and boxing and won the medal for top average at shooting. I was Captain of the House boxing and shooting. (I was recently able to note my name for shooting on the board now up in the girls House that took on the name St Aidan's, after it was closed down – but no sign of boxing!) The excitement of all these sports helped my enjoyment of school tremendously. Often matches entailed travel away for the day and sometimes for the night, which added to the fun and a break from school routine. So, I was lucky.

I felt sorry for those who were no good at games; the emphasis at Public schools in those days being definitely on sport. Games for us took place on four afternoons a week with Corps (military training) on two and one afternoon for scouts or beagling in season. Ampleforth had its own pack. So, for anyone unsporty or unadventurous, even if gifted for study, life could have been very dull. But enjoying games amongst ourselves, or better still playing for the school, was a tremendous boost. Perhaps my own best individual effort was in my last year in the boxing ring in a contest against Newcastle Grammar school. I was the heavyweight to take the last bout of the afternoon. I had already spied from my classroom window the group of Newcastle boys outside on arrival in the morning, to see who the biggest thug was to be my opponent. Our contest came last with the scores then level, so all depended on me. I started with fists flying with no opposition in the first of the three rounds and the first half of the second. Then feeling on top, I let my guard down to receive a stunning blow on the chin. Luckily the referee was our own PT instructor, who told my opponent to stand back. It gave me time to recover. We resumed with me a bit more wary. I lasted the match and then to my great joy and loud cheers from the school, I was declared the winner and the match was won. A great hero, I was given my colours later that day.

The Sea Scouts, whom I joined for their Wednesday afternoon outings, were run by Fr Jerome Lambert. He was a law unto himself. We were definitely the outlaws of the school. Fr Terence was very suspicious of the Sea Scouts, but when I mentioned to him that this all taught us initiative, I could see he mellowed a bit. Little did he know what we got up to and what I had meant by initiative. We had a den behind the lavatories. Sailing was done on the Gilling lakes across the valley. It was here on that first frozen Christmas holiday, staying at Swathgill, that Jerome, as we more often called him, showed his daring, taking his jalopy across the ice. I was to learn my sailing there. On whole holidays we often camped on the banks of the river Rye above Helmsley. Here we were to catch fish, but not necessarily by orthodox methods. Scattered around the countryside, preparing for the invasion of France, were Nissen huts filled with ammunition completely unguarded. Amongst them were boxes of hand grenades. Jerome "helped himself" to one of these to bring to our camp. On the first occasion Ralph May and I were given the task of throwing one into a deep pool. But just as we had taken out the catch to prime them, someone shouted that a soldier was coming down the river from a nearby camp. Grasping the spring of the grenade tightly in our pockets, we chatted with the soldier for several minutes until he went off back again. With great relief, we threw our grenades into the water. There was then great joy, after a muffled woof and splash, when up came lots of dead fish, about twenty – mostly grayling. Later that evening, Jerome was to boast to his uncle Fr Sebastian Lambert, then Housemaster of Cuthberts. He, also a keen fly fisherman, had thought he had done rather well that day with two or three fine trout from the Ampleforth valley stream. He looked rather askance at Jerome's fish and wondered why some of them looked a bit battered. "Oh", said Jerome, "they must have been foul hooked." On another occasion, fishing on the Isle of Mull in August 1945, I threw a Mills bomb into a burn and up came a dead otter.

Jerome left a legacy of many good tales. Two are worth telling. The first was the incident of the whale. He claimed he shot one with a 22-rifle as it was swimming off the shore on Islay. The other was his capture of a German spy, also while on Islay. Jerome became very suspicious of a man he met on the island who claimed he was there as a bird watcher. But when Jerome questioned him about birds, he obviously hadn't a clue. It was more likely that his binoculars were trained on the convoys passing between Islay and Northern Ireland. Jerome reported him to the police; he was taken to the Tower of London and no doubt shot.

At another camp at Yearsley reservoir on the eve of D-day with the sky thundering through the night with the sound of planes, I was to do the most remarkable feat. We were walking across a field, Bob Campbell and I, when out of a bush in the middle flew a cock pheasant low in front of us. With the instinct of a fly half rushing forward to catch a ball from the scrum, I did the same to catch the surprised pheasant in mid-air. It was soon plucked and in a biscuit tin over our campfire. No matter that it was right out of season.

Another exciting scout holiday took place on the Solent in the week before Christmas 1943. Scattered around on their moorings were landing barges waiting for D-day. The general public were forbidden to sail but for the Ampleforth Sea Scouts it was different. Jerome had managed to get us recognised under some naval title, so we were allowed. We were housed aboard one of the many yachts moored in the river Hamble for the duration. (How cold it was sleeping!) We had several one-ton yachts at our disposal. I was put in charge of one, feeling very inexperienced, having only sailed a few times in dinghies on the Gilling lakes. But somehow, despite the tidal conditions, I got by. Jerome decided to sail with his three senior boys, Bob Campbell, Ralph May and me, to the Isle of Wight and stay the night at Quarr Abbey. He had once spent time there touching up his French with the French monks before teaching. Off we set across what seemed to me a vast stretch of water, as if we were crossing the Atlantic to some far-off land. We moored at Cowes and bussed to the Abbey, where we were given a great reception. That evening at supper I had an embarrassing moment, sitting at the guest table in front of the abbot. I had accepted a large helping of seconds of pudding, then to realise I was the only one eating. With the abbot and whole community waiting, I wolfed it down as fast as I could. With a smile on his face the abbot then rang the bell for grace. The next morning a thick fog came down. We went to our yacht but there was no hope of setting off, so we returned to the abbey for a second night. The same thing happened the next day. I was beginning to wonder how the junior boys left on the Hamble were getting on alone. No appearance of worry from Jerome. They certainly were learning initiative. The third morning the fog cleared. It was a lovely day for the sail back to base. It was time to pack up and to train home. I found myself chatting on my own in a carriage with a delightful girl, but that is another story.

Cards sent home described all this:

**Shalimar,** *Bursledon*

*Log Friday. Heaved out of bunk 7.30 am. At 8.10am good breakfast on Zitan. 11 am Get aboard yacht Zenocrate. Start engine. Steam against wind and tide down Hamble to Southampton Water. Wind Fresh SW. Sail around down towards the Isle of Wight. Cook lunch on primus in cabin. No waves of any size. Wind dies down 4 pm when at mouth of Hamble. Sail with a light wind against ebbing tide. Engine conks out. Very slow progress. Met up with and towed back to ship. Supper. Bed. Cont. Saturday. Wind increased violently in night from SSW. Sail in charge of May out against wind and tide. Have to take in a reef and tack whole way. Very slow progress, 3 hours (12-15) when at mouth. Wind stronger outside and highest waves. Tiller doesn't answer very well in it. Nearly run aground once! I'm properly out. Wind begins to slacken. Cook lunch. Steak, potatoes. Take out reef. Sun comes out, blue sky. Marvellous sailing ½ way to Southampton, then back half-way to Isle of Wight. Sail with Zwinst back to Hamble mouth.*

**Quarr Abbey,** *Isle of Wight*

*Monday Dec 15th, 1944*

*This is where I am spending the night on our voyage to the Isle of Wight. There are just the four of us, Fr Jerome, two others and myself. Setting out at 10 we came here in Zenocrate and arrived Cowes 12.30. We enquired of the Traffic Control Officer and found good anchorage further up inside the harbour. The four men from the sea rowed in their dinghy to the shore and walked in their oilskins and Southwesters to the bus stop (with not too sure legs) and bussed the seven miles here. At this French Abbey we are being met up with real monastic ceremony. Already I have been introduced to the cows and allowed to milk one. Except for one or two monks they all speak French, and I am getting on très bien. We eat in their refectory with them, and to-morrow we pull up anchor and sail back to the Hamble and up to Bursledon.*

There were other camps at the beginning of the summer holidays earlier in my time on the Isle of Islay, where the scouts went equally wild. I went on one. The boys brought with them any of their guns from home or school, 12 bores, 4-tens, 22s. We used to blaze away. On one occasion on the moor a bird flew up, I shot and down it came. Bob Campbell, a true Scot and sportsman, shouted as I proudly held it up, "Put it down, Hopkins. It's a grouse. It's not the 12th of August yet." It was delicious, roasted on our fire that night. On another occasion as four or five of us were prowling around a moor, out of a gulley just in front of us rose a great stag. We fired away with all our guns, but to no effect. Again on Mull, seals looked up at us from just below some low cliffs on the edge of the sea. Another blast from us just seemed to make the seals even more curious.

The owner of the farmhouse on Mull, where we lodged in the outbuildings that July/August in 1945, was recently from London, and Jerome thought him completely clueless on field sports. So, he told him near the end of our fortnight that due to the endless sunny weather, it was no use trying to catch the salmon with the fly anymore. We must net them. This was the way we had caught numerous fish off the beach on Islay. We could see these huge salmon in the pools in the burn near the house. The nets went in, and were gradually brought to the side. When near it was a great sight to see some of the smaller boys jumping in and clutching a salmon to their chests almost as big as themselves. On our last evening we cast our net at the mouth of this burn, where from a waterfall at the top on the cliff, it ran in an estuary for a hundred yards across the beach. With the lack of rain in the past two weeks the sea trout had been unable to get up the waterfall. With the net across the mouth several of us thrashed down the estuary. We then brought in the net to find we had caught around 120 sea trout. This, we were told, was a record for the island. I hardly dare tell this tale to a friend now visiting the island and finding just a few fish for his rod.

The other sport we had was out on the Sound of Mull in the evening in rowing boats. We had a plank across for two to sit on and two poles each with goose feathers attached to the hooks on the line. We would see the guillemots diving in the distance, then row frantically to find the sea seething. In no time we would catch some 100 saithe and cuddy. These went to the Irish workers on the farm, who dried them in the sun to eat through the winter. With the sea trout we each took two home with us, wrapped in a dock leaf. In the hot weather mine, after 24 hours travel, were to arrive home rather smelly. To crown the bliss of this scout holiday came the news near the end that Japan had capitulated and the whole war was over, but not without a feeling of uneasiness at the way it had happened.

In that last term in the interim of the capitulations in the two theatres of war, I met up with my cousin Elsie Cholmeley and her husband Eppy staying with my Aunt Alice at Swathgill. They had just returned from China with a dramatic tale to tell. Being on Hong Kong Island at the time of the Japanese invasion in 1941, they were immediately interned. With barbed wire separating them from the beach they spotted an upturned boat lying there. Within a few days they managed to crawl under the wire with one other man and drift through the night to the mainland. They were the only ones to escape. First getting through to the Portuguese enclave of Macao and then the Japanese lines, they reached the communists in the North. They married. Being of very left-wing inclination they returned to work for the communist regime in Peking, editing an English magazine and doing other good works. For their pains they were later imprisoned in solitary confinement for two years in the Red Revolution. Seeing Elsie on returning briefly to England after her release she was a completely changed person – shattered. She and Eppy both died in China.

Work did actually come into the equation at school. Our first target was the School Certificate at the end of the second year. I managed to get credits in all my subjects, but just a pass in maths. Study for the Higher Certificate then began. Greek began to get more difficult when you had to compose verse. From a letter to my father early in my second year from Fr Bernard, the careers master, they thought I was good enough to get a scholarship in classics to Oxford. I think my early promise then began to fade. But it was in the Christmas holidays that, encouraged by my father, I decided to go for a career in medicine. This meant turning to science. One big reason for leaping at my father's suggestion was I was still fighting against that urge to join the priesthood or the monastery. This seemed my way out. It was a great relief. But brought up on classics one always felt science was much inferior. I don't think this helped in all my early medically-orientated exams, until I reached the clinical stage. This at any rate was my excuse for my failures. But I was soon to score one brilliant success. Joining a class, who had been doing physics for over a year, at the end of the first term I won the form prize. Perhaps it was the novelty. I took the 1st MB exam the first step in the medical school ladder, in my last summer term. It was a dismal failure. But I had already been accepted in any case for the Middlesex Hospital Medical School in London. Entry in those days was nothing like as difficult as later. In my interview with the Dean he seemed only interested in my ability to play rugby.

And so, having celebrated VE (Victory in Europe) day May 1945 earlier that term with a large bonfire beside the 1st XV pitch, I came to the end of my last term at Ampleforth. I was very sad. This feeling to my amazement was shared even by those from the non-games players, who all along had hated school, or 'shack', as we called it. I had my two leaving interviews, one an extra one from my biology master Fr Anthony Ainscough as I was going into medicine, and then from Fr Terence. In the first I was told the facts of life. He made it all so attractive, I couldn't wait to get married. I left Fr Terence with ringing in my ears – "You've done really well Christopher (the first use of my Christian name)" and "Marry a Catholic."

My overall assessment of my time at Ampleforth was that I accepted our renowned Headmaster Fr Paul's dictum – that we were to be Catholic Gentlemen. Like the majority of my fellow Amplefordians of the time, I left with a great love of the place. This was largely due to the monks who played such a dominant part in those halcyon days. They were a great bunch. I have to say in my day there was a great lack of the feminine touch. Was that good for us? In our last years we certainly had a great longing to meet girls. How fortunate the school is now!

Leaving, I didn't want to lose my attachment, and revisited my Alma Mater yearly for many years, albeit on occasions to take on the school at rugger. I became very fond of Fr Terence, who I felt was a second father to me until he died twelve years after I left. We corresponded frequently and he married Mary and me. He was to send me a telegram in my second year at medical school inviting me to join him for a cricket match at Lords

– signed 'Tintax'. When up for a cricket match against the school in the summer of 1957, I visited him in his room in the monastery, where he was then confined in the last stages of emphysema (he was a heavy smoker). I was told how he said that dying was the best thing they did at Ampleforth. After he died later that year Fr Hubert (Popeye) sent me a large photo of him. He knew my attachment. One felt a great bond with all the monks, who did the majority of the teaching and were all the Housemasters. Apart from the latter none of the others really took part in the discipline of the school, so one didn't have to fear them. In fact, discipline was definitely in the hands of the senior boys, the monitors. This could have its downside, as already explained, but it was good for developing leadership. Ampleforth in my time definitely left most of us strong and devout Catholics. I have to admit, if I ever felt tempted not to toe the line, in the immediate years after leaving, what kept me there was "must not let my school down" (I can hear my own laughing at this). Of course, home upbringing also comes into it. So, from shortly after war was declared in September 1939 until the capitulation of Japan in August 1945, these were to be those most formative years of my life, all spent at Ampleforth.

## The Effects of the War

How in fact did the war affect me? Apart from being dislodged from our home in Rochester and never having any permanent house of our own for the next four years, what effect did it have on my morale and fears and what contact did I have with the onslaught on Britain from the air?

As with the majority of civilians, for the most part one carried on with the daily concerns of life. For a boy it was schooling and getting on with one's peers. But one couldn't ignore or be unconcerned with the news and the running of the war. After Dunkirk until the entry of America into the war we felt very alone even with Russia's entry. About the most depressing time was the fall of Singapore when Japan entered the conflict in December 1941, and the loss of our most cherished battleship the Prince of Wales shortly after. It was only Churchill who kept our spirits up. But somehow we also got by with the help of the weekly comic half hour radio show *Itma*, songs such as *Run, Rabbit, Run* and films such as *Mrs Miniver*. The troops' spirits were certainly raised by the singer Vera Lynn. I couldn't see how we could possibly win the war. Hope only rose with our victories in the desert and the breakout from the Normandy beachhead.

Although away from London for the most part of the war, we always seemed to return there when things started hotting up. First when the Battle of Britain reached London in September 1940, as already recounted, and then to buy a house in Hampstead Garden Suburb in 1943 in time for the V1s and V2s. I returned home for the holidays. It was in the Christmas holiday in 1940/41, lying in bed at night on our Warwickshire farm, hearing the *ziz ziz ziz* of the German bombers passing overhead on their way to Coventry, that produced a chill down my spine. After several nights of this, a very terror-stricken family appeared in their car in a lane near the farm gates to sleep overnight fleeing from the Blitz.

I can only speak of living in the North West of London where the two weapons only slightly affected the area. Just next to us on the Heath extension was an anti-aircraft battery. I remember them firing off just once. After the all clear from a raid, one bit of fun, rather like picking up conkers, was finding shrapnel in the streets from the anti-aircraft fire. Some of the women crew manning the guns, members of the ATS (Auxiliary Territorial Service), were billeted in a commandeered house round the corner from us. Passing by one day, one of two ATS at the window I heard saying to the other, "There goes your boyfriend." Longing as I was to take this up, I was far too timid to do so.

My father also acted as part of London's air defence. Situated at the other end of Hampstead Heath was a rocket site manned by the Home Guard. As one of them, my father went on duty once a fortnight, sleeping overnight with others in a Nissen hut. Only once was he called to fire his rocket. He had no idea of the result. He had a tendency to snore. He made us laugh relating how on one occasion not getting off to sleep he heard a voice in the dark saying, "Is Two-Stroke dead?" An incident he also told us about that rather excited the adolescent me. It was a buzz bomb, or doodle bug as they were also called, that landed in the Strand outside his office and blew the clothes off a girl.

At one time my father also did duty as a fire watcher on the roof of a building near Westminster Cathedral. It amused him when the warden in charge always described an imminent air raid as 'eminent'. My father thought the fellow was obviously influenced by the proximity of the Cathedral's Cardinal. While on Hampstead Heath a V1 pilotless aircraft came flying past. As it wasn't heading for me it wasn't frightening. When the detonation of a V2 rocket went off it was all over. No one usually saw them coming down. At their onset the authorities kept us in the dark for a time as to the cause of the explosions in order not to give any aid to the enemy as to where they had landed. They were explained as domestic gas explosions. I was again on Hampstead Heath when a rocket landed a mile away, shaking the snow off the trees around me.

At night we went to sleep in a Morrison shelter, a solid metal table with room under it for four to five people. Set up in our hall we felt safe from the buzz bombs. They came over more frequently at night. Hearing the buzz of the plane while inside, if the noise suddenly stopped you held your breath until the noise of the explosion came with relief. I found it all rather exciting as you felt the chance of a direct hit was very small. It gave a pleasant adrenaline rush rather like doing a bungee jump. At any rate living in our part of London the pilotless onslaught that was supposed to terrorise the population had no effect on me.

Rationing and the blackout were all a bit of a pain, but bearable. You dreamt of lashings of butter, sweets galore and the lifting of food restrictions, that even after the war seemed to be going on forever. We never went hungry! We did help our food sources by "digging for victory", the end of the Heath extension being set aside for allotments. I became a very enthusiastic vegetable gardener and encouraged my father to take on three plots, spending much of my holidays there. What I wanted to hear about from home during the school term the most was how the tomatoes, beans or carrots were doing. I was able to continue this passion on buying our present residence Ford House as it had enough land to have a large kitchen garden. I have to say, in declining years this is now much reduced in size.

Staying on farms in the first part of the war, I was also able to see how agriculture aided the war effort. At first on my uncle Hugh's farm, run by my cousin Richard, tractors had not yet been introduced. I remember Richard saying that tractors would never last. "They will compound the soil," he said.

The farm at Wolverton in Warwickshire, where we stayed from 1941, was more up to date with tractors, but milking was still done by hand. I did my bit on holidays milking the nearly dried-up Jersey cow. The farmer did his own bottling and supplied the village. However, little did the villagers realise how the creamiest of bottles were left on their doorsteps. I heard from my young sister Rosemary, who accompanied the farmer's daughter Dune on her rounds, how she took the caps off the bottles and gave them a good lick.

Harvest time was a joyous occasion, with half the village joining in. Refreshments, including my first taste of cider, were brought to the field. Then came the fun of chasing the rabbits as they ran out from the ever-diminishing patch of corn. Making a bit of money doing the stooking of the wheat sheaves could have its painful side, as so many fields then were full of thistles – nothing like the unblemished fields of today.

# PART TWO
# UNIVERSITY

# Middlesex Hospital
## Medical School 1945-52

This was first written in 2011, in my 84th year. Some dates and events, I excused myself, were bound to be confused. (I don't think in fact they were!) It was written with my grandchildren then mostly adolescent very much in mind. Looking back, what were the salient features of the time between entering the Middlesex Hospital Medical School in October 1945 and finally qualifying as a doctor in November 1952?

Firstly, the grind of my studies and facing the fearsome obstacles of exams. The Finals exam was the only one I passed first time. I was to fail on four occasions in between. Now over sixty years later I am still having recurring nightmares about sitting those exams again.

Secondly, all the many exciting adventures on the way. One benefit of failing several exams in the early preclinical stage before reaching the wards was that terms were interspersed with long vacations, time to get away to explore what was then within one's reach in the post-war world, Europe and the surrounding seas.

Thirdly, sport. This meant rugby, which was the cause of real rivalry between the London Medical Schools, culminating each season with the excitement of the inter-Hospital Cup.

Fourthly, the social life, which meant the attraction of girls, more sophisticatedly referred to as women. Having come straight from an all boys' monastic boarding school, I had a lot to learn. At seventeen, coming up eighteen, I was yet to kiss a girl, and yearning to do so. The Middlesex didn't admit women until two years later. But of course there were nurses.

My first year was to see me struggling to get through the first hurdle 1st MB. This comprised Chemistry, Physics and Biology – all sciences which I tended to look down on from my earlier classical education, which didn't help my application to my medical studies. Staying at home in Hampstead Garden Suburb I travelled daily on the underground to the Middlesex in Soho. Having been going backward and forward to school for six years it was a great relief to at last be permanently living at our comfortable home. It was so nice to be in the bosom of my family again – my father, mother, and sister Rosemary, younger than me by seven years, and my dear Aunt Hilda. I was to make two good friends in that first year and lost both. One, Peter Shipsey, from failing the exam, and the other, Jock Campbell, dying of leukaemia, a month short of taking it. Peter and I, after donating our blood in vain, saw him off at Golders Green Crematorium. I managed to just scrape through the exam, being referred in Biology and being allowed to retake it in December.

The winter saw me enjoying my first taste of Hospital rugger in the Extra A team. It was also my first experience after the game of drinking beer in any quantity and singing bawdy songs. This started in our huge communal bath with increasing volume through the evening. I found them amusing to begin with, but then rather repetitive. Perhaps the most amusing part of it was seeing Peter's elder brother, Mervyn, a year ahead of us in the school, covering up their kid brother's ears at the more genital parts after coming to watch the match. Peter used to like telling his dirty jokes. He teased me later that in my naivety they used to make me blush.

When was I going to find my first girl to kiss? I went along in my first term to one of the nurses' weekly hops in their home at the back of the Hospital. I became friendly with one nurse and then invited her to a long walk in the Chilterns and back home to tea. She was very nice, but not the most encouraging girl to make that first step. I was definitely put off by my mother from ever asking a girl home again, when for some sort of protective reason she started to pour scorn on her when she left. I didn't continue. Peter did his best to get us both going. He arranged for us to meet up with two quite attractive ex-convent schoolgirls from his locality Beckenham – the Wainwright sisters Patsy and Maureen, one a red head the other dark. We met at the cinema on several occasions and for a dance at Christmas. I was shy, the atmosphere stilted and awkward. I gave up.

My chance came at last in the New Year. Invited by a friend, Charles Hodgson (destined for the stage) to join him, I went to a Finchley Convent Old Girls' dance. There I met an attractive and easy-looking girl who I then invited, with Charles, to my first party at home. Nothing doing then but inviting her to a cinema later and seeing her off on the platform at Victoria Station, at last I had that small brief peck through the carriage window. I was on my way.

Before misleading anyone as to my views and practice on the moral code, let me make myself clear. My views at that time I feel sure were shared by the majority of my friends and acquaintances, whether of religious belief or not. We looked with disfavour and regarded as immoral anyone who practised sex outside of marriage. (One of the few exceptions I knew was a bishop's son.) Celibacy, of course, was enhanced by the fear of pregnancy. This all changed in the sixties with the pill, which produced the so-called sexual revolution. But to my mind there is something lost by all this. I am sure there was an excitement as well as that greater romantic feeling between the sexes that existed more strongly then. (I was pleased to see recently in the press some research which showed how much more pleasurable sex was for those who abstained before marriage). At any rate I can say I obeyed the Queensberry rules – nothing below the belt.

At the start of my first summer vacation, in a heat wave, I was riding my bicycle the hundred miles to my Aunt and Uncle in Leicester. There were not so many cars on the roads in those days, so it was possible. But with the heat and lack of training I arrived exhausted. From Leicester I went on by train to visit my old school, Ampleforth. I had already made one visit in my first term away, partly out of devilment to visit my big school chum, Michael Hardy, who was having one more term there, to 'patronise' him. My thoughts and feelings were in fact still there. On this second visit I was invited to join the Old Boys' Cricket tour, staying at the Prep school, Gilling Castle, starting just after the end of term a week later. This I did, joining with another old school friend Bob Campbell, who had just finished after one more year. My main recollection of the tour was sitting out games in the rain, and the monks on the tour, Frs. Peter and Dennis, having fun giving me my first real taste of wine in the evenings on the roof of the Castle. At the end Bob invited me to stay at his home in Scotland. Being from a rather pukka family, Bob had to make excuses for me not having my black tie for dinner. But we had some enjoyable trout fishing, tennis, my first turn behind the wheel on the road with Bob (no driving licence!) and meeting his two charming sisters. Back at Leicester, joined by my father, we had a very pleasant tour on bicycles of the Peak District. Lunching each day at a pub, we had the satisfaction of beating the locals at their own game – dominoes.

At the end of August my father's job in the Exchequer and Audit Department of the Civil Service took him for an inspection to Northern Ireland. My mother, sister Rosemary, Auntie Hilda and I went with him. On the eve of the journey out, dining at Michael Hardy's Uncle and Aunt, his Uncle Corney generously gave me my fare, after I mentioned that I, the poor student, was going to save by bicycling the first hundred miles to the Midlands. We stayed in a small hotel in Bangor, just outside Belfast. As fortune had it, also stationed at Belfast at the time, in the Army but still privates, were my school mates, Michael Hardy and Giles Foster. (Both later became godfathers to our children – Michael to our second daughter, Giles to our eldest son.) It was good to see them both and to look round Belfast with them on their off duty. Being told that the bullet holes from the 'troubles' of 1922 were still to be seen on some walls, I blessed the fact that it was aeons in the past and wouldn't happen again now in my time.

I had planned to tour the whole of Ireland on my bicycle and visit some of my Irish friends. At Ampleforth we had a contingent of some fifty Irish boys coming from Eire every term. The English connection amongst the middle class was still strong then and Irish education not considered good enough. I had already arranged to stay with two, John Ryan in Limerick and Owen Heape near Cork. But such is the generosity and hospitality of the Irish that on my three- to four-week tour I only stayed at paid accommodation on five nights.

I set off on my bicycle from Bangor to spend my first night at a Youth Hostel on the coast under the Mourne Mountains. The next day I cycled along Carlingford Lough, past Warrenpoint to Newry. I pictured that road years later when a whole convoy of British soldiers was murdered there by the IRA. At Newry I decided to avoid the long road to my next destination, Dublin, by taking the train. Arriving there in the early evening, I attempted to phone my first hoped-for contact, Donal Cunningham, to beg a bed for the night. Not finding him, I managed to phone the Ampleforth monk, Fr. Hubert (Popeye). I knew he stayed every holiday with his mother in Dublin to escort the Irish boys at the beginning and end of each holiday. Travel was not so easy then. It was said he made the best of his stay on the racecourse. Fr. Hubert told me that it was no use asking Donal's mother (whose husband was the fashionable gynaecologist in town) to sleep on her French sofa. She wouldn't have allowed it, but I could stay with him. So there I made my way to find also staying my old headmaster, the towering Fr. Paul. It was sweet to experience my first Irish household, saying the rosary together on the upstairs landing before bed.

My next port of call was John Ryan at Scarteen, Knocklong near Tipperary. It was too far to cycle in one day so I had one night on the way at Portlaoise. I was to make one bloomer that day by ordering a meal of ham on a Friday. Seeing the large mouth-watering spread that the waiter brought (coming straight from rationed Britain as I had), I suddenly realized the day. The proprietor quite understood, when I asked to change it to an omelet. 'It made me feel at one with them, even though I was an Englishman.'

After passing through Tipperary on the Saturday afternoon, where it seemed full of tipsy Irishmen having spent their week's wages at the bars, I at last arrived down the drive to the Ryans' old family country home, Scarteen. As with many similar Irish families, it was obviously hard making ends meet. They farmed, and also staying to help out were two students from the Continent, as paying guests. The Ryans had their own pack of hounds, the well-known black and tans, from which the notorious British soldiery of the 1920s took their name. Thady, John's elder brother, the master of the hunt, was very keen that I should stay to go on their first cub hunt. I was foolishly equally keen, though at that time a very inexperienced rider. I often wonder how I would have got on over those banks.

But the continuous wet weather had delayed the harvest so the first day kept being postponed. At any rate I did have a ride round the fields on Thady's well-behaved hunter. In the evenings I encouraged the party to play dominoes, but my winning all the time after my success in the Peak District, I was told this was bad form. I was also in John's bad books when on lending me his .22 rifle I shot a rook on a tree by his house at some 70 yards. It would bring bad luck he said. (He, poor chap, died of cancer quite young.) I was the pillion rider on his motorbike for Sunday Mass next day. At meals it was my first sight for years of large piles of butter, so I made the most of it. I was enjoying this, the young company, the hope of going on the hunt, when after the fourth night John's mother asked through him how long I was going to stay. I am sure she was worrying about her budget. So it was time to move on.

My plan was to go south and on to the Ring of Kerry. On my behalf, the Ryans kindly phoned their cousins who lived in their large old family country house on the shores of Lake Killarney. In their turn to help funds they had turned it into The Country Club Hotel. They were descendants of Dan O'Connell, the famous Irish politician. I was getting into my stride, now cycling through the sparsely inhabited Irish countryside. There was very little traffic. Not infrequently on the roadside, I was appalled to pass hovels (the cabins), with the poor dwellers in squalor, seemingly sharing them with their poultry and animals.

I had a great reception by the cousins, taking me in, a complete stranger. There was a mother and father and a most attractive daughter of my own age, and no other guests. It was a nice evening, one of the rare ones that season. I strolled in the gathering darkness with the daughter on the shores of Lake Killarney. Perhaps she was lonely in this isolated spot; I could feel the vibes between us. Many years later in the 90s I managed, after a bit of difficulty, to find my way down that long wooded drive to the house to find no one at home, the door up the front steps open with rows of green gum boots of all sizes just inside the porch. No one answered the bell. "Who lives here now?" I wondered. Perhaps that daughter with a large family?

I moved on the next day. I offered to pay. I felt I had to as it was a hotel, but of course they refused to accept. I do hope I wrote to thank them. It was then the Ring of Kerry ahead of me, travelling the coast anti-clockwise. I passed through some very dreary small towns before reaching Waterville and its hotel the Butler's Arms for the night. I had heard it was famous for its sea trout fishing. No doubt it was good, but I still had memories of the 120 we had caught with the Ampleforth sea scouts on Mull the year before.

The East side of the Ring, facing on to the Kenmare River, became less bleak and more attractive. It was when chatting with a man walking along the road next day that I learned the feelings of the locals around there during the war. "You know," he said, "many round here in the war wanted Hitler to win." I reached the attractive village of Sneem, halfway down the inlet, and decided to stay awhile. There was a small pub on the side of the green, which charged ten shillings (50p) a day all-in. I felt I could afford that for a short time on the £20 I had started with. But to stay any time I needed to find some work. I asked the very pleasant land-lady, who did her best to help, suggesting that I could join a gang digging a trench. She also told me of her experience of the Black and Tans, how a rough lot of them had burst into the pub threatening her. But they were quickly followed by their officer, who ordered them out. Staying at the pub was a lady whose daughter lived nearby married to a retired English brigadier. She also knew a well-to-do family who had a farm whose sons had been to Ampleforth. She thought they would be sympathetic and she would take me there. That was the next day.

So after looking in on a ceilidh that evening at the village hall across the green and Mass in the church next morning, we drove to the family farm a mile or two away. I explained a haystack in a barn was all I wanted to sleep on. They apologised but as they had two French girls staying with them it just wasn't on to have a man sleeping on the property. "You know what the French are like!"

The good lady then took me to her daughter for tea. After a pleasant chat the daughter told me she would be delighted for me to stay there. They had a young niece of my age coming to stay the next day, from London, so I would help to entertain her. It all sounded very good. My Ampleforth credentials had been my password. They lived in a very pretty house down a long drive on the shores of Kenmare River. There was a tennis court and a sailing dinghy moored at their jetty. I really had landed on my feet. The niece arrived the next day. She was a very pleasant girl, not the amenable or kissable sort but very easy to get on with. We played tennis and I took her out in the dinghy on the Kenmare River. We also had some fishing and a duck shoot. At night we started with a dinner party in the house, with plenty of drinks, then off to the 5 Star Parknasilla Hotel, a couple of miles away to dance. It was all great fun. The brigadier's wife was charming, still youthful and renowned as the beauty on the Irish racecourse. I was sorry to leave.

It seemed a long weary way after passing through Kenmare town, along the lonely countryside on the road to Cork. I was on my way to stay with Owen Heape and his mother living in the country to the North of it. By this time I was getting quite adept at getting a lift along the road, hanging on to the back of lorries. The weather as usual was raining and the roads muddy, so I was getting sprayed and mud spattered. There was very little other traffic, so there was little problem hanging onto the outside of the open lorries of those days and being bowled along at speeds of twenty miles or so. The drivers never seemed to mind.

About lunchtime I came to a particularly lonely spot at the top of a small pass. There was an isolated farmstead on the side of the road. Being accustomed from school days on the edge of the Yorkshire moors to calling on farms for a meal, I knocked on the door. A terrified looking woman answered it, peering over her shoulder at my request. A gruff man's voice from inside said, "Come in". I entered straight into a parlour with a large table down the middle and seated on a bench round the walls five rough looking men. I was sat at the top of the table as the woman went out into the kitchen. Silence – five pairs of eyes staring at me, then from the one who appeared the chief: "Are you in the British Army?" He may have spotted the khaki bag holding my things on the rear of my bike.

"No, I'm a medical student," I spluttered out. I should have added, "and I'm not a Protestant."

"You know we are about to kill a pig on that table" the chief went on. Chilled, I wondered if this meant me or the real thing. The women came in with a plateful of bacon and egg. With difficulty I managed to swallow the bacon, leave half a crown on the table, hurry out and away on my bike, much relieved.

Passing to the north west of Cork there was a sign to Blarney Castle a little way off the road. I debated whether it would be a good chance to improve my reserve in speaking, by kissing the stone, but time was passing. In the early evening I arrived at the house in a small village at the address that my old school friend, Owen Heape, had given me. Two elderly ladies answered the door, Owen's maiden aunts, to explain that Owen and his mother had moved to another house over the mountain, some twenty miles away. Despite my mud-spattered look they invited me to stay the night. It was far too late to go any further. I was shown to their spotless bathroom to clean up. Then after a good meal and much refreshed, I went to bed.

After an easy journey for me over the mountain the next morning, I made it to my proper destination. I stayed the night. Asking them whether there was a good cheap place to stay at on my next step back to Dublin along the east coast, they said the Trappist monastery of Mount Mellory.

I arrived there in the afternoon to be greeted by the guest master who started to show me round the separate guest house. There was a modest fee attached. But when I mentioned my Ampleforth connection he insisted that I stay in the monastery itself for free. I was delighted but felt some sort of qualms when on walking down the corridor inside, we met the abbot, who immediately asked if I was the new novice. I felt trapped. It was an enclosed order. I was a bit surprised that evening looking round the supper table at my fellow guests at how rough they looked. Not the sort I thought who would be making a spiritual journey, well not that one anyway. It was only later I was told they were all alcoholics staying there to be sobered up. I felt a temporary sense of freedom when the next afternoon I found that a door in the garden wall could be opened and I escaped for a walk up the Knockmealdown Mountains, just behind the monastery. There I surprised a fox walking towards me. It stopped, made a circle around me until it was down wind, gave a sniff and then was off. I crept surreptitiously back into my monastery.

The next leg of my journey was around 100 miles to Dublin. I must have been really fit by this time as the ride, without any hitches that day, went with no great effort. I bicycled into Dublin city and managed this time to contact Donal. He apologised that there was no question of staying with him, but he had found me a cheap lodging for the night. We met up later and also by chance, as I was cycling to the station the next morning, I bumped into him again. Donal was to meet my future wife at a house party in England, while I was away skiing, just before we became engaged. He asked if he could give her a good night kiss in bed. She agreed. I am sure Donal was as trustworthy as me, so that was it. He poor fellow was one of the unfortunates I had to witness when I was a monitor at school in St Aidan's being beaten.

I reached Belfast to catch the overnight boat back to Heysham, and from there the train home to London. On meeting up with my Irish friend, Mervyn Shipsey (his brother Peter had been called up into the army by then) at the start of the autumn term at the Middlesex, I was able to crow about my adventures over a large part of his homeland, to compare with his own stay just at his family origins at Waterford.

I started the autumn term with only Biology to concentrate on. In my other important engagement, rugger, I was now promoted to the 'A' XV. This was captained by another old Ampleforth boy, Bill Barry. His twin brother, Pat, was also at the Middlesex. In early November we caught the evening train to York after our Saturday afternoon game, to play for the Old Boys against our school on the Sunday. It was whilst there that my old sea scout master, Fr. Jerome, invited me to join his scout party to ski in Switzerland in the Christmas holidays. I gladly accepted. But I needed to raise the £20 cost of the trip.

My chance came shortly afterwards when the washers-up at the Savoy Hotel went on strike. I was readily taken on for the evenings at two shillings an hour. It was quite a contrast from the smart restaurant above to the steamy washing-up room below. It was all done by hand. The foreman put me on the knives as he felt this appropriate for a medical man. On one evening the management felt the strikers were getting too aggressive and it wasn't safe for us to leave even by the front entrance. They invited two of us to stay the night in one of their hotel suites. Delighted, I felt sure there was a Hollywood film star in the room next door. Lounging in my bath the following morning, with a phone alongside I enjoyed speaking to my parents to explain just where I was. The strike went on long enough to raise the £20.

The Biology exam in December went well, so I was through to start the next stage, the 2nd MB, after Christmas. I returned to the Savoy once more to wash up. It was for one day – the day of the then Princess Elizabeth's wedding. My old foreman gave me a great reception, but made sure we kept quiet to the other dishwashers about my previous visit.

Having faced a threatening enemy across the Channel for six years, crossing the Channel to Calais, followed by a train journey through France and arriving in Switzerland, seemed strange. The French porters still came swarming aboard as soon as you docked shouting, "Porteur, porteur!" so you knew you were abroad. We were told the railway bridges were not yet really safe – the French were so keen to get things going. The overnight train to Basel had frequent stops at stations on the way, with hordes on the platforms trying to get into our compartment. One ruse we used to discourage intruders was at each stop to put a coat over the head of one young scout in the corner and call out "Fièvre jaune!" They looked puzzled and backed away. It was good to put our French into practice after all that classwork. I had more chance when we did allow a young French girl in. She sat next to me and I was quite surprised that it wasn't that difficult to converse, but was nearly overcome by the strong whiff of garlic. I must have made some impression as on one occasion, when I was asleep, the others told me she had asked for my address.

We took a local Swiss train from Basel, and then a funicular up the mountainside to arrive by the early afternoon at the resort of Stoos ob Schwyz. Expecting to find snow at Calais we didn't see it until half-way up the funicular. Stoos was just a very local resort, with only one drag lift. I had had the experience of skiing when we had two weeks of snow in my last year at school, so got into it fairly quickly. But turns are not easy with those old fashioned bindings and boots. On one occasion missing my turn, I fell down a steep bank to land winded on the path below. Unable to move or speak I heard a couple standing over me saying, "Ein Englander." At the small restaurant at the top I had my first taste of gluhwein, definitely the best way to prepare for the descent. It was an incredible feeling looking across a valley at snow-topped mountain peaks and thinking there we were in the heart of Europe, after watching the other way round all those years.

It was at a dance in the small hotel on New Year's Eve that I met my first Swiss girl, Heidi Engeler. A name like Heidi seemed too good to be true. She was good fun and gave me the chance to practise a bit of German as well as French. I did get her address.

January 1947 was to see the coldest and longest spell of wintry weather across Europe for the century. It was to last into March. Back home in Britain, there was a shortage of fuel and power cuts, but one felt sorry for the many refugees still scattered across the Continent. Hospitals were not affected and I spent many of my lunch hours keeping warm in the showers at the swimming pool under the Nurses' Home, the pool itself not being heated. It was reserved for the medical students at this time. Before the arrival of women at the school later in 1947, the custom was not to wear costumes. The matron ordered this to change after seeing myself and another in the water, but oblivious at first, while she was showing a prospective mother around. It was about this time that rationing became its most severe. This included white bread and potatoes, something that hadn't happened even in the war. It seemed as if rationing and austerity would never end.

The cold spell ended, and then after a late spring came the start, by contrast, of the hottest summer. The swimming baths were heated again. I joined our Hospital water polo team as goalie, for the hotly contested inter-Hospital championship. We being the weakest team meant I had much practice in saving goals. It was against St. Mary's that I must have impressed their captain, also captain of the London University team, as I was then asked to join the Varsity for their final against the University of Liverpool, taking place at Liverpool. We won the match and I my University Purple, without having had to stop a single goal. The night was spent at a Temperance Hotel, perhaps to keep us in order. I was asked subsequently in the autumn to join the training team for the Olympics in London the following year. I declined; I wasn't that keen on the sport. Did I lose my one chance of gaining an Olympic medal?

In my medical studies I had started Anatomy, which meant dissecting corpses. The most bizarre part of it seemed to me the irreverent and lewd talk which so often took place amongst dissectors. In charge of the anatomy department was a Professor Kirk, a very dour Scotsman, who treated us with a rod of iron. If he felt we were falling behind at all he would call you in for an interview and ask, "Are you sure you have a vocation? Was it not just the idea of your father?" I lied and said yes to the first and no to the second. I was glad I did. I have not regretted it since.

Answering an advert in the Evening Standard for a second rank rugby team to tour the Channel Islands, Bill Barry's 'A' XV arrived by boat on Jersey at the Easter weekend 1947. It was interesting to visit the only bit of British soil to be occupied by the Germans during the war. We were billeted among the families of the Jersey team. Playing the match on a damp afternoon I can only remember the result as close. The rain persisted and by the time we were due to transfer to Guernsey their ground was waterlogged, and the match was cancelled. We only saw Guernsey from the sea. The return journey to Weymouth was most exhilarating. The waves were enormous, but as it was brilliant sunshine, sitting out on the stern of the ship was fun, watching one moment the bow of the ship high above you and the next looking down from a great height. It was a foretaste of crossing that part of the Channel several times later under sail.

Back home I took Mervyn Shipsey and Austin Tuohy, both in the rugger team, for their introduction to sailing at Burnham on Crouch. The United Hospitals had just opened the Sailing Club there after the war. We were the first to launch the ill-fated dinghy Oyster Catcher into the water. The wooden hull promptly filled with water before the planks sealed up. In quite strong winds we sailed madly up and down the Crouch just as far as the mouth. Only a few weeks later two students took Oyster Catcher into the open sea up the coast; sadly, it capsized, and one was drowned.

The summer term ended and the long summer vacation began. My first priority was to earn money to enable me to go off somewhere. I rode my bicycle down into town with the idea of calling on the Savoy to work in the washing-up department again. Cycling down Wardour Street in Soho, the heart of the film industry, it suddenly struck me: why not try to be a film extra? After one enquiry I was advised to report to the office of the Film Artists' Association in nearby Beak Street to get my Union Card. I was told this was run by a woman called Miss Bacon and I was to go in and say, "Hiya Streaky." I joined the queue out in the street. The man in front of me told me they were casting for some filming the next day. My turn came to stand in front of the desk with Streaky and another man behind. They looked up at me without asking me anything and said to each other, "Yes, he will do as an Italian waiter". It was for a film called Snowbound at the Pinewood Studios. My union card was immediately given and with a great deal of excitement I reported at Pinewood next morning at 6 a.m. Pay was two guineas a day, which seemed quite a nice amount to me. My part was to join in some shouting in a crowd in a hotel trapped by the snow. This went on for 5-6 days. The British film industry was booming then, and for all of August I was turning up at one studio or another on most days. One week, I signed on for a fairground scene, which went on through the night. I needed to get some sleep as I was also working in the day. With another fellow we hid at the top of the spiral helter-skelter. Hearing noises which sounded like the studio police coming up the inside stairs to seek us out, we waited until they were near to the top, and then slid on our mats down the outside spiral chute. I made the enormous sum to me of £20 that week.

It had hilarious moments. At Shepperton Studios making a Carry On film, the extras were in a luggage compartment on a train bringing Welsh rugby supporters up to London. We had to form a scrum and pretend someone's bowler hat was a rugby ball. It amused me that many of the extras felt we should be getting danger money. I felt quite good coming forward to give some expertise on how to scrimmage, but received no extra reward.

I had a great ambition to get onto a film on horseback. To improve my expertise, I hired a horse from the Bull and Bush stables up the road. I cantered it madly round and round the track on the Heath extension, thinking myself a cowboy. It was a really hot day. When I returned the horse to the stable, very lathered up, the owner was furious as he "wouldn't be able to hire it out again for the rest of the day". But sadly my hopes came to nothing. The studios closed down for a holiday at the end of August, but by then I was well in pocket. It was my time to get away.

Earlier in the holiday, I had biked down to Pembrokeshire with Mervyn to join my family on holiday there. We stopped off on the way for a night or two at Oxford, where Owen Heape, studying medicine put us up in his digs. Walking back from a dance we had one bit of fun. Passing through Parson's Meadow in the dark we found a mixed party bathing in the nude. We hid their pile of clothes in the bushes, and then ensued a battle when they discovered their loss. It was my one and only time to wrestle with a naked woman. In the latter part of our journey, thumbing a passing lorry, it stopped, loaded us and our bikes aboard and took us a good 100 miles on our way. This gave me the idea that if you could hitch-hike with bikes, how easy it would be without. So, in early September, with Switzerland my target, I was on my way.

I landed at Ostend from Dover, intending at this stage to avoid as much of France as possible, still not recovered from the war. Belgium was already looking prosperous, on the other hand, and overflowing with food, serving large portions of meat on a restaurant plate. My first night I slept in a Youth Hostel in Ghent, then on through Brussels to Luxembourg. Getting lifts was no difficulty. I arrived in front of the huge gates to Prince John of Luxembourg's palace. He was an old boy not only of Ampleforth, but also my house, five years or so before my time. Should I knock at the gates and ask for lodging? The formidable guards in stylish uniform at the entrance put me off and I slunk away to the Youth Hostel. For once my courage had failed. Thinking back, John, after fighting through the war in the Guards, would probably have welcomed me in.

I took public transport next morning to the frontier with France and waited. The frontier guards were most co-operative when I asked if they would find a car that was going all the way to Basel. It wasn't long before there was. He was a very pleasant Luxembourg man called Reuter. He was pleased when he heard I was called Christopher as he felt I could protect him. One thing that worried him was German prisoners of war escaping from camps in France. It was now over two years since the end of hostilities but there were still prisoners. Passing through the French countryside it looked parched. It had been a long, hot summer and no rain. We reached Basel at nightfall, where I again found my way to a Youth Hostel.

From Brussels, I had sent a card to Heidi, whom I had met skiing, to say I was on my way. She lived with her parents in Zurich. Everywhere looked so clean and smart compared with shabby France, as I hitched my way along the route. It was getting very hot. On arrival the Engeler family gave me a great welcome and invited me to stay. After a cooling bathe in the Zurich See in the afternoon with Heidi, others came to join us in the evening at the family home. They all wanted to plan my route round Switzerland. So next day I hitched without too much trouble to the Swiss/Italian border at Splugen to stay at the Youth Hostel there. The mountain scenery along the route and at the border was magnificent.

At Sunday Mass the following day in the pretty little village church, I embarrassed myself. Arriving early, I found a seat halfway down on the left. As the church filled, I began to realise that all around me were women, giving me funny looks. The men were all on the other side.

My intention then was to go through a bit of Italy by way of Lake Como to reach Lugarno. I made my way over the pass and then had a very hairy descent in an Italian's motor-bike sidecar. He saw my fright and went faster and faster round all the hair-pin bends. I reached the first village and frontier post. I was then told I couldn't enter without a visa, so back over the pass to Splugen I had to go. But not before I had a very enjoyable time in a hotel drinking wine and being the centre of attraction of a party of Italians. So the next day I went by way of the St. Bernard Pass (no sight of any dogs) to Lugarno. The Youth Hostel there was full but they found me a bed on some hay in a barn. The scenery was again beautiful. After failing to get some girls to go with us (they weren't attracted by a false French accent I tried to put on) I went with another man that evening in a motorboat to a dance across the lake. The next morning I was itching terribly from the creatures in the hay.

My next objective was Geneva via Grindelwald. Starting out and walking mile after mile up a valley without a car stopping, I cursed them for being Italian. I vowed if I had a car, I would never not pick anyone up. My morale began to drop. To my rescue in the end came a British officer on leave from Germany, in a rather clapped out Land Rover. We had to traverse the Gottard, Furka and Grimsel passes. The road was narrow and each time another vehicle came along we had to edge past it, with a sheer drop on our outside. My driver admitted his handbrake didn't work, so that he had to rely on the foot brake alone. There were many scary moments. With relief we reach Interlaken and then went up to Grindelwald for the night. The Eiger towered above us. The Jungfrau, just round the corner, had been especially mentioned by Heidi, pointing to a prominent part of herself by way of explanation. After another day's hitch hiking, I reached Geneva, staying at the Youth Hostel there.

I decided I must visit Paris on my way home, but my luck ran out. Waiting at the French border next day I failed to get any lifts and had to spend another night in Geneva. I was more successful the next day, a first lift taking me half-way to Paris, and another the rest of the way. The second was with a young English couple. I was walking along the main street of a town, not a good place to hope for a lift. They passed me for a hundred yards and then stopped. It was a French loaf sticking out from my haversack, the wife said, which made her feel sorry for me. But on the whole, if you were thought to be British, hitch-hiking through Europe in the first few years after the war was quite easy. As recent liberators we were very popular. A Union Jack on your knapsack and wearing a kilt were infallible.

The Youth Hostel in Paris took you in for one night only. After one night in a crowded dormitory, the student agency helped me find some cheap lodging in the Latin Quarter.

It was fascinating to be touring in the city having heard and seen in film and pictures so much about it – the Eiffel Tower, Louvre, Champs Elysée and the Arc de Triomphe. In the evening I just had to see the Folies Bergères. Walking back through the streets afterwards I paid a brief visit to a *boîte* for a strip show. With the shop windows in the Rue de Rivoli seeming to be just full of brassières, I began to feel overwhelmed by breasts. I had had enough. So, taking the train from the Gare du Nord next morning, I sped back to London. It had all been a great experience. But arriving home the Continent had the last say. Hardly back, I developed the most terrible diarrhoea. I blamed it on a peach I couldn't resist eating off a barrow in Paris. France was still looking grubby and dilapidated in the aftermath of the war.

The autumn term began. I was now playing for the Hospital 1st XV. It was in a completely different league of Club rugby. The better hospitals were still being taken on by the best clubs, having kept up their strength during the war. Our fixture list included the excitement of playing Leicester Tigers, Wasps, Northampton, Saracens, R.A.F. and others. Our team included four or five county players and in a later season the hooker for England. It was the amateur game to be enjoyed. But to win always helped. Headlines in the Evening Standard reported that we remained unbeaten in the first two months of that season. But we were usually well beaten by the best teams, such as the Tigers. My Uncle Gill, an old Tiger, was always there to watch, which drew comments in the local rag – known as the 'green-un'.

The spiritual needs of the Catholics started about now to be well looked after in both senses by the Hospital chaplain, Fr. Simpson. He was a late vocation, having been a solicitor, so he was a man of means. We met monthly at his church behind the Hospital in Ogle Street for discussions and to hear speakers. Fr. Simpson was a member of the Spanish Club in Cavendish Square, where on numerous occasions he would take us for a most enjoyable dinner. This was always heavily fortified in his presbytery beforehand with strong doses of gin and Dubonnet. He was acquainted with interesting people such as Graham Greene and Dr Halliday Sutherland. We met the latter at one dinner but never the former. I was amused by the smile brought onto the elderly doctor's face by my asking after the señorita he was obviously attached to during his stay in Spain as a young man, whom he mentions in his autobiography, The Arches of the Years.

In those days there was a certain camaraderie among fellow Catholics, or bead-swingers as we were affectionately called. Most if not all were regular church goers. One of my happiest memories was of meeting up at the last Sunday Mass in the morning following a boisterous party the night before. Today sadly the young don't realize what they miss.

My finances were now being augmented in another way. Following on my extra work, which could only be done in my vacation, I was taken on by several model agencies. The agencies and photographic studios were all conveniently close to the Hospital in the West End, and sessions would only take an hour or two. The most frequent need was for the knitting world of jumpers. But once I was asked to take my evening suit to a house in South London, where I posed in a telephone box in the street outside dressed up with a box of Cadbury's chocolates in my hand. This appeared full page in the Picture Post magazine. Aertex also asked me to pose, one moment in cricket or tennis gear brandishing bat or racquet, the next doing the same exhibiting their underwear. One high class request by Baron, the court photographer, to report to their studio in Park Lane, where I was to do a joint take with a female model, came to nothing. After waiting around in their studio for over an hour I was told I wasn't needed. Did they think I was not up to it? Or did the female take fright? I was paid all the same. I had another trip down the Thames from Tower Bridge to Margate, in a paddle steamer, posing with an accompanying girl, to illustrate the Company's brochure. On another occasion in late summer, when all the public swimming pools had been closed due to fear of the latest Polio epidemic, I was asked to report for a photo shoot at a house conveniently near in Bishop's Avenue with a large pool in the garden. This was to accompany a bunch of lovelies, all in our swimming costumes. I was to cause a bit of a sensation when, getting quite friendly with one particular model, I pushed her into the pool. Her costume was definitely not meant to get wet!

I was also introduced to the embryonic television world at Alexandra Palace. We were bused from the BBC Broadcasting House at Portland Place to be the audience at a weekly live show called Café Continental. I had to sit at a table with my partner watching the floor show, and then we were to dance together. Our sham drinks were completely non-alcoholic, so to get over my nerves of a camera beaming at me and to get the right atmosphere, I freely imbibed several G & Ts at a makeshift bar on the terrace outside before the action started.

In July 1948 I had my first encounter with the 2nd MB exam. I passed in Physiology and failed in Anatomy. This meant I had to take them both again in the following March. Disappointment, yes, but one consolation: more long holidays.

The Summer Vac began. The desire to go to sea and in particular to sail was strong. On the first day of my holiday I had gone down to the Pool of London to the docks to see if I could work my passage. I was told I would first have to get my union ticket. The quickest way was to go on a hairdressing course, which would take four weeks. I thought that was too much to take out of a three months' vacation with the uncertainty of a ship at the end of it, so that wasn't on.

But I was on the crewing list at the Royal Ocean Racing Club. This had already given me one weekend trip earlier, in a city man's luxurious yacht, on the south coast from the Hamble to Poole and back. Then in early August I had a phone call to say I was wanted to join a yacht, the Northern Light, on the race from Brixham to Santander. Before going I just had time with John Bunting to have a day seeing something of the Olympics now under way at the Wembley Stadium. The next afternoon I was on the train to Devon with the owner, Dr Scott, to join the crew of two other doctor brothers Ian and George, an artist named Tiger and his wife, a girl they had picked up at a port of call on their way round from Bristol, and another student Richard. The yacht was a Norwegian Pilot Cutter, sturdy, almost as broad as she was long, definitely a cruiser not a racer. Ocean racing was a more amateur affair then, and many came for the party at the end. This was certainly Northern Light's case.

We steamed into Brixham in the gathering dusk to a hearty reception by the rest of the crew. We ferried out in their pram dinghy to the Northern Light moored far out in the harbour. Loaded heavily and with the gunwales only an inch above the waterline, I wondered if we would make it. The race started the next morning and we slowly rounded Berry Head and were soon trailing most of the thirty or so yachts. There was only a light breeze as we drew away from the coast. I had no idea of the baptism of fire that I was about to experience on my first offshore sail. Here is an account in scrawled handwriting in an exercise book of what happened, from one of the crew:

*Northern Light was two days out from Brixham on the first leg of the Santander race to round d'Oussant. It was evening and we had been heading into a light south-westerly breeze all day. The crew of* seven were sitting idly about the ship, little realizing the night that was before them.

At 5 o'clock the wind began to rise, the sky to the SW darkened at a hideous rate. Tiger was at the helm. The skipper put on the 6 o'clock weather forecast. "Warning to shipping. Gale in sea areas West Channel and Biscay." We knew we were in for it. The wind immediately began to rise. "We had better start reefing," said the skipper. By the time the first reef was brought in on the mainsail, the seas had already mounted, drenching the crew working up forward as the sheets of spray came horizontally across the bows. "Bear away, Tiger. We are getting soaked." A second later, "Look out, you fool. You're gybing her." But too late, the boom swung across with a crash that shook the whole ship from stem to stern. Disastrous this might have been to any lesser ship but the Northern Light was built when ships were built for strength and not beauty.

It was only now that we realized the full force of the wind. As so often happens the reefing has been left too late. The seas were churning through the scuppers as we keeled over with far too much canvas up. "We must take in the rest of the reefs quickly," said the skipper, "and get up the storm gib." The crew struggled to obey on the pitching deck, one hand clinging first to the rigging to save themselves being flung into the angry seas, the other free to work. Eventually all was done, and while the rest of the crew went below, two kept the first night watch.

Darkness descended, the wind increased still further. N.L. held her course heading into the teeth of the gale. Great waves pounded against her sides. To those below it seemed the beams must give way any moment. The noise was terrifying. It sounded as if a thousand ghouls were shrieking up above, and a cannon firing into the ship's sides. There was little sleep for the watch below.

There was a tremendous roar outside, then an almighty crash and a thump, with the ship jerked bodily sideways. There was a shout

*from on deck, then one mass of water cascaded down into the
saloon. The time had come for more dramatic action. "We must
heave her to," said the skipper. The crew adorned their already
sodden oilskins and climbed outside. It was a murky night. After
a great struggle the mizzen was taken in. The helm was put over
and she was hove to. As if by magic the action of the ship was
immediately calmed. One man was left at the helm as we drifted
slowly backwards towards the English coast. The rest of the crew
tumbled into their bunks exhausted. By dawn the storm was over
and the N.L. under full canvas, headed once more southward.*

It was me at solitary watch at the helm. There was nothing to do except
keep a look-out. I could see lights of ships in the dark around us. Luckily
none was menacing as we had no means of steerage.

The storm had a devastating effect on the racing fleet. Many were so
damaged that they had to call into port. Northern Light was probably the
best yacht to weather the storm, but no one was to know that at home.
There was no radio contact in those days. The storm made news. When
one by one all the other yachts arrived at Santander, Northern Light made
headlines as missing. My parents naturally became very anxious. Aunt
Hilda arrived at Paddington Station to see a poster outside the newsa-
gents with "Northern Light still missing" on the board.

Oblivious of all this, we were sailing blithely along in light winds. Off
d'Ouissant at the North West tip of France, we became becalmed, and I
dived in for a swim. It seemed weird with the depth of the water below
me and wondering what creatures might be there. The sail across the notorious Bay of Biscay was blissful with brilliant stars at night, many shooting, and the excitement of passing near a three-master tunny fisherman.
Tiger entertained us with his songs and stories. One in French to a tango
rhythm has stayed with me ever since:

*Je ne suis pas curieux
Mais je voudrais bien savoir
Pourquoi les femmes blondes*

*Ont le poilu noir*
*Et pourquoi les négresses*
*A quatre-vingt-dix ans*
*Ont les longues tresses*
*Comme les éléphants*

It was supposed to be naughty and Tiger only agreed to sing it if I promised I didn't understand French. Land came in sight on the seventh day. We were right on target. As we were approaching Santander harbour, gently bowling along, I put a rope with a lifebuoy at the end, to tow me along. With the warm sun shining it was heaven.

We had a great reception as we tied alongside the harbour wall. The local press photographers came aboard. Lined up on deck we appeared next day on the front page of the Santander *periodico*, labelled as "Los ultimos". The Spaniards were extremely hospitable. There was no official exchange rate in 1948. Spain was still very alienated. But Franco gave £100 worth of pesetas to every yacht that arrived and larger awards to the winners. Each club, the Real Maritimo, Real Hippatico and Real Club de Golf, had a dance with live bands arranged for us every night. I became very friendly with a charming señorita, Chamilla, and also a party who were working for Franco in Madrid. I corresponded with them all afterwards and was invited to stay with the party in Madrid in the Christmas holidays, but sadly couldn't afford the fare. I would have particularly enjoyed the political climate and the romance of Spain (Don Quixote and all that) of those days, lost with the arrival of hordes of tourists. I did see them in London a year or two later. The wine was flowing, so we were very merry. It all helped to swirl my Spanish partner around the floor. The crew slept soundly in their bunks at night, four of us including the girl, in the huge one on the port side, aptly called the 'lust bunk'. Dipping over the side into the sea every morning was the essential way of starting the day. At a restaurant near the quayside I had my first taste of *calamaris in su tinta*. It was delicious.

I invited a party of señoritas on board. Going below I am sure they thought it rather sordid. Seeing one button missing on my jacket sleeve, they excused it by saying it must have come off in the gale. I greatly admired the elegant way they held their skirts close, climbing their way back up the steep steps to the deck ahead of me.

All too soon it was time to say farewell and head back for England. One had to again endure the first two days of *mal de mer* before regaining one's sea legs. The voyage took another seven days. We encountered one storm in mid-Biscay but not severe enough to heave to. Sailing in the sunshine afterwards with the huge rollers that had developed was most exhilarating, one moment in a trough, then lifted as if to the top of a mountain. They were as big as houses. For some reason after a while the sea appeared like a huge field where I expected to see cattle grazing. Navigation again was just by a log trailed behind and intermittent fixes with the sextant. One thing we had to endure on the return voyage was the monotonous food. On the way out we had used up all the more delicious varieties. On the way back we seemed to be only left with tins of grade 3 salmon. I never wanted to see salmon again. On the seventh day the skipper asked me to climb the mast and look out. He was bang on. There was the Wolf Rock lighthouse off Land's End dead ahead.

We rounded Land's End and crept up the west coast until in the evening we were off Minehead. We anchored there close to the shore, then to land and have our first taste of beer in the pub after our week at sea. Ian phoned a friend in Bristol to meet us at the quayside at Avonmouth the next morning to collect two cases of Spanish brandy, bought at 5 shillings a bottle (25p). In hardly any wind we drifted through the night up the Bristol Channel, arriving at early dawn off the quayside. I was given the job of rowing Ian ashore with the two cases. With the deserted quayside looming high above I expected customs officers to appear at any moment on the skyline. Instead, after heaving the cases to the top, within moments the friend's car arrived, the cases were loaded and he was away. I was away myself soon after to join up with my family on holiday in Pembrokeshire and a great reunion.

The autumn and winter came and with it more rugger and parties. Both were going well. In November I celebrated my 21st birthday. Starting at home we finished up at the Coconut Grove night club in Regent Street. I had been previously introduced to it at someone else's 21st in the summer. The night clubs were the most exciting places at this time in one's life and, if you didn't buy drinks there, surprisingly inexpensive. So you went well fortified. At the Coconut Grove in the dark sensual atmosphere you shuffled around, squeezed tightly to your partner on the packed postage stamp-sized floor to strains of Edmundo Ross's South American band. Many other parties and dances took place, including the annual Hospital Ball in Park Lane. I had lost my inhibitions about the opposite sex by this time and was enjoying myself. At one time I totted up the number of girls I had kissed to 17 before I lost count. How does this compare with a recent boast of a Lib-Dem leader that he had bedded 38 at his time at Oxford?

In the Christmas holidays I had my second skiing holiday with the Ampleforth sea scouts at Kandersteg in Switzerland. It again involved much trudging in the snow as there was only one small ski lift. We again enjoyed seeing the New Year in at the local hotel with the young Swiss but met no Heidi this time.

March 1949 was to see my second attempt at 2nd MB end the other way round – a pass in Anatomy and fail in Physiology. My despair and shame was profound. Not daring to break the news on returning home, I left the tube at Hampstead to walk back over the Heath. I couldn't have cared if the buses coming down the hill ran over me. Unknown to me dear Mervyn had already phoned my parents to help by breaking the news. I picture it now the four of us standing in the drawing room, my sad looking young sister Rosemary sideling against me. But the despondency was short lived. Summer came and with it more adventures.

Experienced as I had become from the Santander race, I was now much in demand at the Royal Ocean Racing Club. I crewed first with one of the fleet on passage from the Solent to Harwich. This was over the weekend before Whitsun in preparation for the annual Harwich-Hook of Holland race, a week later. It was a pleasant, easy and rapid sail round the Kent coast, catching the flood tide up the Channel in time for the ebb going north off the Foreland. Getting into Harwich in the dark, the sea became a picturesque sight with the lights on the masts of numerous trawlermen around us.

Crewing on the Hook race a week later in another yacht proved to be a quite different affair. The yacht *Colona* was owned by a pleasant but elderly couple. Also crewing was my fellow Middlesex student, Peter Hunt (Peter's widowed mother was later to be my patient at Southwold. His father had been the Methodist minister there). All started peacefully, as the fleet sailed close to the Suffolk shore on the first evening, passing Aldeburgh and Southwold. It must have been a fine sight as seen from the shore as I often picture it now nostalgically. On the first leg we had to round the lightship N2 about halfway to Norway. This we did with the wind increasing the following day. A storm developed which soon became too much for the owners, and we were hove to. We drifted on with the couple staying below and Peter and myself left on deck until the wind abated many hours later. The wind turned very light from the west. The couple had had enough and decided to head home. But after many hours of seeming to be going nowhere, just due South and North, Peter and I, desperate to make land abroad, pleaded with the owners to make it somewhere on the Continent. We altered course to head SE with no knowledge of where we were, as we hadn't taken any readings. After a few hours in this direction we spotted a fishing boat that was about to cross our bows. Taking note of the port of origin on the stern – it was Ostend – and then a bearing of the direction it was heading, our skipper made the most amazing fix. Altering course on this information, we sailed on. Twelve hours later we came dead on the Hook buoy and were up-river to the Rotterdam Yacht Club, just in time for the celebratory dinner. The owners of Colona were then going on a cruise of the Dutch inland waters, so as our studies called us, Peter and I hitched a lift back home on Erivale, the winner of the Santander race. Another feat of navigation impressed me, entering the Crouch on the Essex coast in the dark without any lights or navigation buoys, zigzagging across the estuary taking soundings. It was this experience that probably saved my life and others many years later, as a party consisting of me and four children, made our way in my dinghy in a thick fog across Iken Broad.

Despite these interruptions, taking 2nd MB again in July (my final chance), I at last succeeded. It left a nice glow inside me to start the long summer vac, knowing I would at its end be starting what I had really come to the Middlesex for – learning medicine in the wards.

But within a few days of at last passing, I was to nearly lose my life at sea. I was asked to crew on the Portsmouth-Dinard race. The course was to leave the Channel Isles to port. After a rough crossing of the Channel, while then cruising down the west coast of Guernsey, the tired skipper took to his bunk below. This left me and an Oxford student, who had never been to sea before, in charge. Passing the southern tip of Guernsey, this clever student decided to do a navigational fix. He didn't get Herm and Sark right and put us already south of Jersey. Coming back on deck the skipper accepted this without question, so when a coastline came ahead we assumed this was France, where we turn left for Dinard. Then everything went wrong. Buoys we passed didn't respond as we thought on the chart. Dusk was setting in. The skipper reassured us that with the surrounding navigational lights soon going on, we would then be able to rectify our position. But nothing corresponded. We cursed the French, saying if only we were in British waters. At one moment, passing near a winking offshore buoy it suddenly went red. We held our breath waiting for the crunch, but luckily nothing happened. It felt incredible to be lost and that one couldn't just ask a policeman the way. After a moment of panic, I began to see the funny side. After all my efforts finally passing 2nd MB, I was to perish within days. We drifted with the tide along the coast through the night. We finally put down anchor at dawn off the Cotentin Peninsular, and all slept. On waking, the skipper realized our gross mistake. We sailed on down the coast of Jersey (the wrong side) to reach Dinard. A naval officer on board as crew had stayed in his bunk all night in a big funk. He refused to come back with us and took the plane home. The passage home by contrast was blissful. We glided across the Channel in sunshine, listening to the Test Match. Off Chichester Harbour, our base, it became very hot, and nearly becalmed, I dived over the side into a balmy sea.

With John Bunting, another old school friend of mine who lived not far away in Barnet, we planned to get away on the Continent. But how were we to go about it? As luck would have it, John spotted an old Rolls Royce, 1925 vintage, converted into a truck, up for auction on a bomb site in Soho. With another old Amplefordian, Tim Odonni, in on it as well as me, John went to the sale. John had previously told the auctioneer that we were interested up to £40. The bids started, stopped at £39, and the auctioneer then declared it was John's. He wasn't quite sure if he had been had or not. The bonnet was locked. We hadn't even seen if it had an engine. I crawled under it and verified there was. In fact, the only thing wrong was a flat battery, soon charged. I was now a proud third-part owner of my first car, a Rolls.

With John, also an impecunious student (in art), Tim a little more flush, we needed more help to travel abroad. We intended it to be a bit of a pilgrimage, starting first at Lourdes, then on to Santiago de Compostela and Fatima. Three others, including Michael Nolan, came with us as far as Lourdes. (Michael was John's cousin, also an Old Amplefordian, later made a peer and author of the Nolan Report.) Despite protests, John made them pay their share of the car's cross-sea passage, both ways. "It has to come back, even if not with you." Two other friends of John's came all the way. So, eight up, the back of the truck loaded with camping gear and our belongings, five on the back and three inside the cab, we set off for Dover in late August, the springs creaking on every corner. I hadn't taken my driving test so couldn't officially take the wheel. This lay on the shoulders of John and Tim.

The only passage available was Dover-Ostend. We looked proudly on, in the way it was done then, at our Rolls being lifted from the quayside by crane into the hold. For our first few nights we put up on farmers' fields or farmyards. Passing through Normandy the wrecks of tanks from the war still lay by the wayside. We off-loaded the three at Lourdes, said our prayers, and then the five made our way to the coast at Biarritz. In a field we put up our tent for the last time.

"This is a truck. Not allowed in Spain," said the guard. Desperate, I attacked the guard with all the Spanish I could muster, from having studied it after the Santander race. "Franco is our friend," I said. "He gave me pesetas, when I came to Santander by yacht last year." "Propaganda," said the guard, and let us through. We were brought to a whistle stop by another Spanish policeman, with his funny helmet, a few miles inside Spain. We had gone the wrong way around a circle in the road. He demanded money. I went completely dumb, answering in English. A crowd gathered but no-one could interpret. The guard became fed up in the end and let us drive on, passing through San Sebastian, Bilbao and then on to Santander.

It was good to be back. On the way to visiting my señorita, Chamella, we met her in the street. After arranging to meet her in the town that evening, she didn't turn up. No doubt it was lack of a chaperone. We visited the Maritimo Club of happy memory, bathed and then slept on the beach. To anyone we met we were staying at the Hotel Playa (beach).

Leaving Santander, we visited the famous Altamira pre-historic caves. A very gracious lady living in a large house nearby showed us round. The drawings of animals on the walls were still in wonderful condition. We had the place to ourselves. Since then, with the booming tourist industry, for their preservation, the caves have been closed to the public.

We followed the coast road on to Xijon and then Coruna. For many miles the road was in a state of being built up, obviously preparing for the much-hoped-for tourists. At that time GB cars were few and far between, just one or two a day. On passing we would wave to each other, like ships at sea.

At Xijon several incidents occurred. First, walking down the main street beside the Rolls, wearing my shorts (it was very hot), a policeman hauled me into his station saying this was not allowed. I was made to put on my long trousers there and then. But the police did come to my rescue as this part of a card from Coruna to my Aunt Hilda explains: *Lost my passport and wallet in Xijon, and created quite a commotion before finding them at the police Station, with half the town joining in. The police seemed very suspicious of us altogether, especially as Franco was visiting the town that evening. We seem to be preceding him round Spain as he is due here tonight as well. He will soon be becoming jealous of the reception we generally get.*

From Coruna we went on to visit Santiago de Compostela with its wonderful cathedral. On a rare visit to a restaurant in the city for lunch, we got involved in another fracas. Before ordering it, we made sure what the price of the meal would be. The owner, pointing to each of us in turn, said "tres" (three). Settling at the end we paid him 15 pesetas, to which he said no, it was 45 pesetas. Annoyed, we asked an explanation. The owner said three was in another denomination, three times in value. We felt cheated and refused to pay. He took us to a nearby police station to settle the matter. Summoning again all my best Spanish I argued my case in front of the officer. He took the Spaniard's side. We were suspicious. We felt sure he was his brother-in-law.

Fatima in Portugal was our next destination. It looked a rather desolate site, with a church at the end of a flattened out rough area the size of a football pitch. Like the pilgrims of old we hoped we received a few more graces.

We debated whether to head off from there direct to Madrid. But before I had left home, speaking to my parish priest, Canon Thornton, I mentioned I was hoping to get to Lisbon. He insisted that we call on and stay at the English College there that had been his seminary. This was a relic of the days of Catholic persecution in Britain, when priests had to be trained abroad. I mentioned to the party that it would be worth the 100 miles to go further on to Lisbon. Having slept rough since leaving England, except for one night in a hostel at Lourdes, the prospect of a bed was tempting. We went on.

Making our way through the streets of Lisbon we eventually found ourselves in front of the door of the College and rang the bell. My heart sank when on asking the priest who came out "Could we stay there", he said. "Sorry, we are not a hotel." But then I used the magic words, Canon Thornton. His expression changed and we were ushered in. Three nights of bliss followed, sleeping in the sick bay, being fed and enjoying their wine from their own vineyard across the Tagus. The Principal was extremely friendly and escorted us around the city. We visited the adjoining fashionable seaside resort of Estoril and bathed further up the coast in the Atlantic rollers. It was a good refreshing rest half-way on our trip in distance and time.

We started on the torrid road to Madrid. The country at the frontier was bare and deserted and remained so along most of the route. At the Spanish frontier post, the officials demanded a large payment and then kept us waiting outside. It was getting dark, so we started the engine and roared off into the night, not stopping for many miles. There was no one to be seen anywhere, as we slept further on by the roadside.

We reached the centre of Madrid and found a school to sleep in, not for the first time. We all paid a visit to a barber, for a cut-throat shave, finishing with a stinging but refreshing good dab of Eau de Cologne. Visiting the Prado museum, we admired its Goyas. At every stop we always took care on leaving the Rolls to take the flying lady statue on the bonnet with us. It was worth we reckoned as much as the car itself.

We left Madrid and headed for the coast at Barcelona. En route we discovered that Saragossa had been another place of pilgrimage. It was our fourth. At this stage, passing through the region of some of the bitterest fighting in the Civil War, we came across a small town still completely devastated and in ruins. On one occasion, taking the wheel without any experience, I very nearly crashed the precious Rolls, narrowly missing a milestone on a corner. The good old truck with its distinctive horizontal front grill had served us well. It only gave us two troubles: a puncture, and on another occasion the cable from the battery getting tangled round the driving shaft. Was it fortuitous or was our puncture anything to do with the garage nearby? We did have trouble starting the engine, so whenever possible stopped at the top of a slope.

After the hot dusty journey across the centre of Spain it was good to get to the coast again. We first tried to be put up at the monastery of Montserrat, outside Barcelona. There was no possibility. It seemed the same at all religious establishments, especially in Portugal. So much for monastic hospitality. We settled on the beach at the north end of Barcelona. Across the road, wine was being sold from a shop with a row of barrels extending down each side. We were invited to taste as many barrels as we liked before deciding on a litre bottle. With a cup each we tried not a few barrels. By the time we had decided, we were well away. That part of town was in fiesta, with bunting (how apt) fluttering from the buildings. We joined in the spirit but had to suffer for it next morning. It was extremely hot. But with the sea at hand it was easy to have refreshing dips. That afternoon we had our first experience of the bullring. I had mixed feelings, but it was all part of the Spanish scene that we had to see before at last leaving the country.

We crossed into France and made our way through the Central Massif on our way to Paris. The contrast in temperature was extreme with us all shivering in the open at night. John had an Uncle living in Paris, who entertained us all for lunch. It was then just a question of making our way to Ostend in Belgium and the sea crossing back to blighty. I had brought with me all the way from England packets of coffee beans which I was told was good currency in France. There was still a great shortage. I had waited to get the best price, and at our last stop in France, sold it off at the very last moment – my one effort at marketeering.

Back home we had to decide what to do with our beloved Rolls. We were fearful of the expense of keeping her. To make it pay we did a bit of furniture removing. At the end of a dance that John, Tim and I had organized at the Catholic Plater Club in Belgravia, that we named the Buntod Hop, we did do a bit of taxi work. Also coming out of the Club, but not at our hop, was Evelyn Waugh. He told us he wanted to get to his White's Club. He accepted our offer of a lift and squeezed into the cab between John and me. He was his usual pompous self. We didn't ask for a fare and he didn't give us a tip.

We made one last journey in it up to Ampleforth and back, to take part in the Old Boys' rugger match against the school. In one mad moment, too tempted, I took the wheel, drove it on my own to the village a mile away and back, still quite without a licence. As we planned our return journey, a boy asked for a lift back to London on the outside; the poor chap arrived shivering. We sold the Rolls in the end to two fellows for £100 – a good profit! We heard later that celebrating on their way home, leaving it outside a pub in Surrey, they neglected to remove the Lady. Coming outside after their celebrations, it had gone.

## Beginning on the Wards

In October after a short introductory course I started my first contact with patients in the wards and at outpatients. We had to clerk the patients, taking histories and examining them in preparation for ward rounds by the high and mighty consultants. At other times we attended the outpatients. On the surgical side we assisted at operations. It could be daunting experiencing everything for the first time. One amazing job for the students then was to do blood grouping and cross-matching blood for patients, all on a small bench in a corridor in the basement. I never heard of anything going wrong. Slowly we gained experience. It was a three-year course. Simultaneously we had lectures on Pathology and Pharmacy.

Christmas came and more parties. It was at a party in Chelsea after Christmas that I met Ingrid and fell deeply in love. She was blonde, petite and pretty with a sensuous husky voice and all the glamour of being an actress. On the first day of the holiday I had walked into the Arts Theatre in the West End and was taken on as one of many assistant stage managers. They were preparing for the Christmas show, Curlew River, which needed a lot of props. We helped to make these up and did functions such as raising and lowering the curtain, scenery changing and much else. On one occasion the actors were about to talk at the beginning of a scene, when there was a huge resounding bang above them. I had rather overdone raising the curtain. I stayed for some two weeks.

As luck would have it, on the night of the Chelsea Party I was invited with all the other stagehands at the Arts Theatre to attend a party there. So pleased that I could show I had something to do with the stage, and having made my first advances on Ingrid, I invited her to join me there at the end of the party. She accepted. Feeling very elated, I ordered a taxi. Managing the bar at the Arts Theatre was Sigmund Freud's grandson, Clement. He was most genial then but didn't somehow want to be reminded of his barman days when I met him again many years later as the holiday family doctor in Walberswick. After a few drinks, Ingrid and I explored the interior of the theatre. We made our way on stage and there had our first passionate kiss. We made our way to the stalls to continue. I was bowled over.

We arranged to meet next day at a bus stop in Piccadilly. I was ten feet in the air. Having some record tokens to spend we were able to have some privacy in a booth at the HMV shop in Sloane Street. We continued to meet for tea at intervals in the sitting-room of the house in Chelsea, where Ingrid lodged with a bachelor 20 years older than herself and his mother. She both wondered at my restraint, and how I could have learnt to kiss at a monastic school. She was doing repertory at the Windsor Theatre, where she invited me to watch her evening performance, one Saturday after playing rugger. We were lucky to have a compartment to ourselves on the train back. In town we joined up with a party taking place at a Hospital hostel near Marble Arch. There we met some of my mates. Ingrid soon spotted, after they learned she was an actress, that they had different ideas in their heads than mine. But soon afterward she phoned to say she couldn't continue. She was obviously finding our relationship frustrating. I was devastated, but then a few days later a call to say she regretted having said it. With the emotional swings it was never quite the same again. Not long after, she moved away to join the repertory company in Birmingham.

However, my life continued happily through late winter and spring, enjoying my medical studies and rugby. March was the time of the exciting inter-Hospital cup matches at Richmond. We won through the preliminary rounds but then met our match against London Hospital. As a stand-off I just missed my moment of glory to win by missing the posts by inches with a drop kick. It was a draw, and then in the replay we were beaten. I did get my come back later playing for the United Hospitals against the victorious county of the time, Eastern Counties, scoring with a solo run from midfield the winning try. Another great moment in my rugby life was to play in the Middlesex sevens. Getting through our games in the preliminary rounds the week before, we again won two more rounds on the second Saturday. This led us for our next game on to the very hallowed turf in the Twickenham stadium itself. It seemed like a vast prairie. Although we lost, we acquitted ourselves reasonably well against the team that made it to the semi-finals.

I was lucky to escape any serious injury in my rugby career, just two relatively minor mishaps. The first, water on the knee, kept me out of the game for a few weeks. During this time, we had a fixture against Sandhurst where my school pal, Michael, was at the time. He was also crocked, so we both frustratingly had to watch the game from the touchline instead of opposing each other. Still heavily bandaged a week later, going to watch Mervyn and Austin Tuohy playing for the Old Boys against their school, St. Edmunds, Ware, they persuaded me to make up the XV. By the end of the game, all the swelling had gone. So much for the advice of the Hospital sports clinic (set up for the Olympics) to wait for the swelling to go down before playing. Much later I fractured my nose on the bald head of Johnny

Schofield, a fellow student, as we both bent down to pick up a ball at the same time. My father was to joke, after it had been set (much improved), that the surgeon had obviously looked round the theatre and modelled it on the prettiest nurse there.

Another sport that I enjoyed especially as it could be very sociable was tennis. Within a year or two after the war we were lucky enough to resurrect a tennis court in between the houses behind us, with the help of a grant from the Hampstead Garden Trust. It had been there before the war. My father being a very good club player from pre-war days, was behind it all, and formed a small club. It became a great asset being able to invite friends of both sexes to play there and have some very enjoyable parties.

I took to the seas again in February, an unusual time to sail. This was after Peter Haward, a professional yacht deliverer, arrived at the medical school out of the blue looking for a crew. He had started his career straight from the Services after the war with no experience of sailing. Peter was one of the first to install harnesses for his crew after losing someone alone on deck off Southwold. He was to give me a lot of fun. This time he was making a passage in a Brixham Trawler, Alassie, from the Hamble on the Solent to Heysham in Lancashire. I joined him with Peter Hunt. Being mid-winter we had to seek shelter from storms twice, first at Yarmouth on the Isle of Wight and then at Plymouth. After rounding Land's End we had an exhilarating sail with a strong wind on the quarter driving us past the Bristol Channel and up the Irish Sea. She was a sturdy boat. On deck at the wheel, we had to dress with multiple layers, while down below in the saloon we kept cosy with a continuous fire burning in the stove. Rounding Anglesey for the last leg we were nearly becalmed, and the temperature became uncannily balmy as we drifted into Heysham. The new owners received us almost as heroes. They had no intention themselves of sailing out of season.

With the summer came my one and only experience of the debutante world by invitation of my old school friend Bob Campbell's sister, Fiona. I was invited to a dinner party at the house in Belgravia that Fiona's mother had rented for the season, then to a drinks party at a house overlooking Hyde Park. There it was interesting to see in the flesh all the Society people one heard about in the gossip columns in the press. Finally, I went to a dance in Park Lane, where you signed all your partners up for the evening. I signed on Antonia Pakenham, daughter of the Labour Peer, there in another party, for one dance. As she lived with her family in my neighbourhood in Hampstead Garden Suburb, I had met her at a local party a few months previously and monopolized her for the evening. She had just left St. Mary's, Ascot, very demure but very interesting to talk to. I escorted her home. We exchanged glances subsequently at Sunday Mass. But that was it. I didn't feel up to taking on this particular Peer's daughter and anyway I had fallen in love a night or two before. On meeting Antonia again at the Cheltenham Literary festival many years later, on lining up to buy her book "The Gunpowder Plot", I asked if she remembered that medical student. I was puzzled by the anger in her voice when she said, "Yes, but he had black hair." What did it mean?

In June I was off in the Royal Engineer's yacht, Overlord, on the Dover-Kristiansand race. It was loot from the war. It was definitely a soldier's wind, being aft all the way up the North Sea. We had to spread the genoa sail goose-winged as we had split the spinnaker in the melee before the start. Passing over the Dogger Bank it was the duty of the early morning watch to put out a spinner hook, to immediately catch a good mackerel each for breakfast. On board was a Norwegian who taught us that the Norwegian girls were called Froiken, but you had to be careful how you pronounced it. It could easily mean something rude.

We arrived at Kristiansand in a thunderstorm in the early dawn 5th out of 17. We were to meet up with plenty of Froiken at parties that evening. They all spoke perfect English, although they had never met Englishmen before. We started at the Yacht Club, then moved to Overlord joined by most of the fleet with much boozing and singing. The song that our fair young maiden companions enjoyed the most, as it was so apt, was *Singing in the Rain*. It was pouring down. Partying continued until well past dawn at the house of one of the Norwegian lasses, whose parents had timely just left at 1.00am by boat for Denmark.

The fleet then moved off along the coast to the pretty little town, Arendal, situated at the head of a fjord. We moored in the quayside opposite the one hotel for an equally good reception. It was Mid-summer's Eve. The daughter of the Hotel owner was a beauty, as were all the girls we met. Years later I discovered she was a good friend of my wife's cousin's Norwegian wife, who also came from Arendal. I spent most of the morning in the hotel bath. That evening we were invited to celebrate at the Yacht Club on an island in the middle of the fjord, taking Overlord over there as we planned to sail off in the early hours after the party. There was a bar with plenty of free drinks and a band playing, but no signs of any of the Norwegians. We thought we had been tricked to get us out of the way and made the most of the bar. Then as dusk began boats arrived loaded with the most delightful girls – maybe anything would have looked good, well imbibed as we were – blonde, slim and all in trousers. We danced. I made friends with one in particular who, despite worrying about her fiancé knowing, allowed in the quietness of the island the most heavenly of embraces for a sailor from the sea.

We moved off in the early hours with the dawn well broken. We were missing one of the crew but captured him in time as he was heading for the mainland in a motorboat, with someone's wife taking him to her home. With no motor and barely any wind we drifted down the fjord to the sea. A card home from our next destination, Copenhagen, recounts:

*26/6/50. Successfully reached this port from Arendal last night, after the most wonderful sail through the Skaggerrak and Kattegat. The start down the fjord after the mid-summer's party was quite chaotic. On the way down we got joined by parties of Norwegians in their motorboats, clustering alongside and furthering the 'skols'. We left ahead of the race to have more time here, and so far, no signs of the fleet arriving. This morning I have been looking around this capital, and a fine city it is. Off tomorrow on the next leg to Kiel. Hope to avoid the Russians.*

Nearing the exit from the fjord we came across an outboard craft zigzagging towards us with a very drunk man on board. We managed to get him alongside, turn him round and power us out to the open sea. We finally turned him in the direction of the land and let him go. Passing by

Helsingor Castle, of Hamlet fame, at the entrance to the Copenhagen Strait was another moment of excitement. How little did I realize at that moment how Hamlet was shortly to feature in my life.

For army personnel the more direct route on to Kiel would have put them in danger from being too close to Russian territory, so we sailed back round the island of Zealand. In the yacht harbour at Kiel, Overlord was really back home; it had been kept there when owned by the Luftwaffe. The same German harbourmaster must have been disgusted at the sight of it under the Engineers, badly in need of paint as it was. The Germans were soon put to work, painting, varnishing and mending sail. The garrison commander entertained us ashore at the magnificent Kiel Yacht Club that evening. Well inebriated, he made history. On being invited to step on board Overlord he fell into the drink.

Without an engine we needed a hitch through the Kiel Canal. The standard way was to wave at a passing ship with a bottle of gin, a pound note in hand. It soon succeeded, and we were towed through to Hamburg, into the Elbe and out into the North Sea. Standing on the quay waiting for our hitch I took the opportunity to shake a German by the hand. It was my way of showing we were friends at last. The passage home was stormy in contrast to the way out. The mainsail split. So, under jury-rig we limped back to Dover. It had been a wonderful and eventful trip.

Another chance to go to sea came soon after, from Peter Haward again. This time he wanted my assistance, taking the battered old yacht Amulet from the Hamble in the Solent to Dartmouth. Our average speed for the 100 miles trip was 1 knot. As we crept along the coast, I was spending most of my time mending sail. On landing at Dartmouth, I took the bus to Torquay. Remembering the Hospital was on a cricket tour there I looked them up at the pub, the Hole-in-the-Wall. I was immediately seized upon to join the team as they were short. I hadn't played since my school days. But taking part in the match next day I made the top score. This made them persuade me to stay for the following match next day, but not with the same success.

I had a letter from Ingrid inviting me to visit her at her digs in Birmingham. I was still in love, and so I hitched my way there in late

July. She was sharing a house with other members of the Company. I saw her performing at the Repertory Theatre that evening. We had a meal and returned to the digs to be put up on a sofa in the lounge. I accepted her invitation for a goodnight kiss in bed. I wasn't surprised to find her naked, as she had already told me this was the normal way she slept. Her main concern then was that I would discover she had lost her virginity. It had happened, she explained, riding. But I had no intention of finding out. Then came bitter recriminations that continued next morning and for weeks by letter afterwards. It was the end. We never met alone again. I had no lasting regrets; we were not suited in any way.

Ingrid had been selected by Alec Guiness to play Ophelia in a modern production of Hamlet that he was staging in the West End in late autumn. I went to see it, paying for my seat in the Gods. I had previously seen her at Birmingham after playing for the Hospital Rugby XV against the City in one of the first matches of the season. I went around to the stage door afterwards with John Rymer, a team-mate, to find her looking very wistful.

By amazing coincidence, I met Alec Guinness myself late in September without recognizing him. I was on location as an extra in a park for the film *Kind Hearts and Coronets*, lying on the grass on my own reading a book in the lunch interval. A man came up to speak to me. I remarked on his false nose, thinking he was an extra trying to be clever. We had a very amiable conversation for half an hour. Half-way through he asked if I would like to be an actor and again just before leaving. I said no, I was going to be a doctor. The action started with the man prominent in front. I asked someone who he was, to be told Alec Guinness. I often wondered what would have happened if I had said yes. Was he looking for his Hamlet?

The modern Hamlet wasn't a success and didn't last long. Ingrid married the older man she lodged with next year. I was invited to the marriage, ostensibly I think to meet her younger sister, a bridesmaid. I took her out a couple of times, but although even more beautiful than the elder sister, she didn't attract me. Over the next two years before qualifying I met and enjoyed the friendship, both platonic and otherwise, of several girls. One such was a very pretty secretary in the Hospital, perhaps the prettiest to be seen in the canteen, where we all had lunch. After a chance meeting sitting at the same table, I asked her out. An only child, she was from a rather unstable family (her father was a horse trainer). She mentioned her parents would have terrible rows, then closet themselves in their bedroom for two days. It was on our third or fourth date that waiting at our rendezvous I received a phone call from Saville Row police station asking me to bail her out. She had been caught shop-lifting – an indication of her disturbed mentality. The officer at the station, when I arrived, took me aside very solemnly to say he hoped I wasn't going to marry the girl. She had fought so wildly when they took her in.

I met one of our fellow students, Robyn (nicknamed at the Hospital 'the Honourable Phoebe') at the annual Charity Concert at the Scala Theatre. I was one of the ushers, which meant afterwards you could go backstage to help entertain the actors. There were plenty of free drinks. With quite a lot on board I got very friendly with Robyn. She invited me to stay the night at her parent's home, in place of her previous invite, named Spicer. I awoke next morning with the most terrible hangover, to find her father – the Labour Peer, Lord Strabolgi – alone at the breakfast table. He greeted me with the words: "Are you Spicer, the grocer?" His bit of fun. After Lady Strabolgi came in and placed a boiled egg in front of me, I felt the nausea inside rising to a pitch. I made a hurried excuse and rushed to my bedroom to be violently sick. Robyn's mother was charming, and we always made a joke of it. His Lordship in spats and wing collar went off to the House of Lords. Apart from school, which didn't count, it was my first experience of aristocracy.

I had several other experiences with the family. On a second occasion I was invited to be Robyn's partner at Billy Butlin's dinner dance at a Park Lane hotel. Lord S must have been on the board. We were on the top table, but Billy B never arrived. Robyn was sweet, but to do my duty by her felt I had to have some drink taken. We were each given a bottle in front of us, me gin, she whisky. I had a fair amount of mine, so again having a frail head, had to face the Strabolgi breakfast table next morning feeling very sick.

I was invited to join Robyn with her parents for dinner at the Savoy on the next election night. As the early winners coming up on the screen were mostly Labour, with Strabolgi and wife cheering, the parties on the tables next to us became more and more angry and menacing. Robyn and I had been cheering the Tories. Her father asked me, knowing I was a rugger player, would I defend him. Luckily it wasn't necessary. I was again asked to attend Lord Strabolgi's Eve of Opening of Parliament drinks party at the Savoy, a few weeks later. Labour had squeezed in with a very small majority. Arriving feeling a bit lost but seeing a figure all alone in the centre of the ballroom floor, I felt this was someone I could join. Going up to him it was none other than Clement Attlee himself. His fellow parliamentarians were shunning him as much as the country. Robyn married a year or so later at Eaton Square when I was asked to be an usher.

In August 1951 I was organizing a party at my home, while my parents were away. That afternoon seeing a quite attractive hospital secretary, unknown to me, crossing the front hall, and short of girls, I asked her along. She came. Her name was Gill de Burgh. It was a good party which went on after midnight. I offered Gill a bed for the night and loaned her my pyjamas (I wore them subsequently for a week). To my disgust and annoyance a medical friend (but not a very close one) who had come with a nurse, blockaded himself with her in my Aunt's bedroom. He had broken all my rules and in my own house. I never had anything to do with him again.

This was to start a new relationship with Gill. It was a platonic one. Her uncle, Brigadier Hardy Roberts, was the Hospital Secretary. He lived in style. There followed many invitations with Gill to his drinks parties at his pied-a-terre in London near the Hospital. The highlight the following February was to watch the musical *South Pacific* in the Royal Box at the Haymarket, and afterwards at a very chic private restaurant for dinner. By strange coincidence King George VI and Queen Elizabeth had been in the box the night before, and the night that we were there, the King died.

I used to make it a rule in any relationship to avoid getting too committed and, to prevent anyone getting too attached to me (vainly, perhaps in both senses), make it end at the first anniversary. It was the same with Gill. She did come subsequently to my wedding.

My medical studies were continuing apace, despite the interludes. In February 1951, it was time to get my obstetric experience. I had the thrill of delivering my first baby on home grounds at the Middlesex. The grateful mother asked me my name, so the new-born was called Christopher. Many of our mothers coming from the surrounding district of Soho were Greek Cypriots. Often there was a language difficulty, but one word of Greek we learnt to use was 'Sproxi' – 'push'. It came in very useful.

I then chose, with John Owen (the Bishop's son), to have my month's experience away at the Carmarthen Hospital in Wales. They had a strange set up for calling you at night at the sleeping quarters in a house just across the road. You had a rope tied to your leg, which you dangled out of the window to the street below, to be pulled when the time for delivery had come. But getting fed up with this, I started to tie the rope to my bedclothes. At the first subsequent call, half asleep, I wondered what was happening as I saw my bedding disappearing out of the window. We knew from others before us that the consultant also always gave you the chance of doing an appendicectomy. My letter home explains the result and much else:

> *I don't know that I like Rosemary's* [my young sister] *suggestion of the appendix case going bad, as if any of my cases could! The funny thing is that whereas John's patient's temperature chart is rather like a picture of the Alps, mine is as steady as a rock. Now John and myself really are responsible men. We now form two thirds of the hospital staff and have been given rooms in the hospital accordingly. All except one doctor are away for the rest of the month. The one remaining is two months qualified and only experienced so far in the medical side. So he has employed John and me, as the only residents experienced in surgery, to take over all appendices and such like emergencies!! Nothing unfortunately has come in yet but we have the whole hospital organised. I have delegated myself the charge of the midwifery section, John to the Gynae, and the qualified man to the male block.*

I can't remember anything going amiss.

During my stay at Carmarthen I had the excitement of my old school chum Michael Hardy playing rugby for England at Dublin against Ireland. I had seen quite a lot of him on and off during my student days, as also my

*My parents, Frank and Kitty, on their
wedding day in 1924.*

*My mother on her honeymoon
on the Brittany coast.*

*My father, a 2nd Lieutenant in the Royal Engineers, in World War I.*

*Excursion into the Egyptian Desert with my parents, Anne and a friend, 1932.*

*My father, Anne, our guide and me, aged 8, on top of the Great Pyramid in 1936.*
*Inset: me aged 4.*

*Anne and me on leave on
Hampstead Heath, 1933.*

*Mount Troodos Camp Cyprus 1935
having fun & games.*

*Rochester on holiday with my mother (to the right), Aunt Hilda (to the left), Anne,
Rosemary and dog Peter in 1938.*

*Ampleforth Cricket 1st X1 1945. I am on the far right, front row, with Hardy (Captain) in the centre. McNulty is on the far left of the back row with Campbell third from the right at the back.*

*At the crease – a practice game 1944.*

Gilling L.&N.E.R.
Ampleforth 224

SAINT AIDAN'S HOUSE
AMPLEFORTH COLLEGE
YORK 31ˢᵗ May, '44

Dear Mummy & Daddy,

We have been having some most marvellous hot weather just lately. It really has been hot. For Cricket & swimming it has just been ideal. But for Corps it has been not so good. On one of the hottest days we had to march through the Village, to its other end and back again; nearly 3 miles marching in the broiling sun. It was to raise, patriotism, enthusiasm and funds for the Salute the Soldiers Week. We must have been a fine sight, just dripping with perspiration. But the whole village turned out and mothers with babes in arms stood in doorways to watch us pass, we entered the Village in fine style, marching down the short hill and entering the village to the "Ampleforth" played by the band. All the kiddies were thrilled, of course, and marched up the street alongside the band. We, at any rate, effectively roused the Village from its afternoon siesta, if we did nothing else. We had a competition amongst the four Recruit sections last Monday,

*A letter home – a week before D-Day.*

*1st XV rugby match against Sedbergh School in 1944.
Hardy passing the ball to me.*

*I am on the left facing my opponent
in a boxing match against Newcastle
Grammar School in 1945.*

*The bonfire below the school to celebrate VE
Day, 8th May 1945.*

*At the helm of Amulet on passage from the Hamble to Dartmouth in 1950.*

*Northern Light on arrival at Santander "Les Ultimos".*
*I am at the back towards the left.*

*Arm in arm with Chamilla at festivities at the end of the yacht race*
*to Santander in 1948. A señor from Madrid on the right.*

*The Rolls loaded up outside my house for our continental trip in 1949.*

*Our stay with the Seminarians at the English College, Lisbon.*

*The three owners in the back of the Rolls Royce.*
*Left to right, Tim Odonni, me, and John Bunting.*

other chum Patrick McNulty. However, he contracted TB, entered into a sanatorium and then emigrated to South Africa. The first sign of his illness was coughing up blood after passing the ball to him on my wing playing for the Old Boys against the school. Tuberculosis is what we all feared in the years after the war. Michael, on first leaving school, relied on me to find him his first girl. I managed to procure for him a nice, pretty, buxom member of my parish, Sheila. They got quite friendly. Michael was able to meet her when in London on leave from the Army. He was definitely on his way. Michael married quite young to Elizabeth, I as his best man. I also managed to slip away to be godfather to their son, Christopher, at the christening at York, just before I qualified, Fr. Terence, our old Housemaster, officiating on both occasions.

A request by Peter Haward to crew the yacht *Odette* from Salcombe in Devon to Gibraltar was too much to resist. I joined him there in early May 1951, with Peter Hunt and an art student. It was a yacht owned by the Earl of Stanley of Alderney, to use on his honeymoon with his third wife. The art student changed his mind about coming on the eve of our sail, saw us hoisting sail outside the entrance, and then changed his mind again. He contacted the Navy at Plymouth and managed to persuade them of his need to join the yacht. They supplied a launch, scoured the seas but all in vain; all of which we were to find out later.

We sailed south with the Festival of Britain just starting in London. It was an uneventful passage. What was so restful was between the three of us, each doing four-hour watches on alone, enabled you to have a good sleep eight hours off. Cruising down the coast of Portugal and seeing a large liner heading north a little further out to sea, I was thrilled to read with binoculars the name on her bow. It was the *Moultan*. This was the P&O liner that I was in when last coming up this way, aged 8, on our return journey from Egypt in 1936. It must have been one of its last voyages before being consigned to the scrapyard.

Coming round the corner at Cape St. Vincent into the Bay of Cadiz we could smell the fragrant scent of Southern Spain in the wind. We reached the Straits of Gibraltar as night was falling, with the lights of the Rock and those on the northern coast of Africa both visible. We entered the harbour of Gibraltar and tied up. It was a week since we had left England. Meeting us there at the Rock was a fellow parishioner of Golders Green, Jimmy, serving time in the Navy. He married my first date of all those six years ago, Patsy Wainwright, whom I had introduced him to. Such are the twists and turns of the weave of life which always fascinates me. Jimmy made the yacht *Odette* his personal concern. Later he told me the Earl never turned up to collect it. Perhaps he changed his mind about the marriage.

Peter gave us our fare home in English pounds. We had heard that you had the best rates by far by changing these to pesetas in Gibraltar, which we did, leaving us extra for a stay in Spain. In a book by Dr Halliday Sutherland on his tour of Spain, I had read about the Hospital Central at Seville. I had written to the medical director there for permission to visit, asking for a reply *poste restante* at Gibraltar, as it was too late before we left England. A formidable document in the affirmative awaited me at the Post Office. Peter Hunt and I took the train to Seville. Hotels then varied from £1 de-luxe to 25p two star per night. We chose the latter, with a comfortable room overlooking the central courtyard. We called at the Hospital Central next day where a very courteous doctor, who happily spoke French, took us on a tour. I had a moment of shock, when on being taken into a room with an isolated patient, the doctor explained, "C'est la maladie de la Bible." He had leprosy. In the public wards the patients were fed and attended to by their relatives. Afterwards we were joined by a number of other doctors, who took the opportunity to harangue us about how badly the British were treating Spain. The Labour government had made many hostile statements against Franco. About this time I wrote a letter to the Generalissimo expressing my regrets at his unfair treatment by some of the British press. I was partly guided by Halliday Sutherland's experiences on his recent Spanish tour, which included visiting prisons. After the cruelty on both sides in the Civil war, he was becoming more of a benevolent dictator. It was something that was needed by Spain at that time in their turbulent history. I had a courteous letter from an official in reply. Later, I wrote an account of our visit for the Hospital journal.

We also visited the Seville cathedral and museum. I still cherish a copy of a Murillo painting, painted by an artist in the museum, bought for a few pesetas. In the evening we went to the theatre to see an exciting performance of flamenco dancing by the most famous dancer of the time. Travelling on to Madrid by the cheapest method, the overnight postal train, we arrived in the city in the early morning to find a reasonable hotel and go sightseeing that included the Prado and its Goyas. We particularly enjoyed the Spanish atmosphere sitting at a bar in the centre of the city, sipping Xerez and tasting the tapas. There were very few tourists about. We took the overnight train from Madrid to Paris, crossed over to the Gare du Nord and then onto the Channel and home. Travelling to the coast, Peter and I, swigging at a bottle of *vin rouge*, chatted up a French girl sharing our compartment. We were feeling very elated now finishing off our round trip. I met the *jeune fille* again in London for one more French lesson.

It was not long before I was on the Continent again. My good medical friend, John Schofield, was marrying a Belgian girl in Brussels. Mervyn Shipsey was his best man. I was invited but worried about the fare. Realizing there was an RORC. race from Burnham-on-Crouch to the Hook of Holland just beforehand, I took the train down to Burnham and waited outside the yacht club where a dinner was being held on the eve of the race. The secretary, whom I knew well, tottered out at the end well-oiled. Asking him if he knew anyone needing a crew, he said yes, a naval yacht. A card I wrote home before the race recounted:

> *By the time you read this, I will be away on the bounding main,*
> *somewhere on the North Sea. I am with the Navy this time on*
> *Bor-Kum, a solidly built 25 tonner – loot from World War 2. The*
> *skipper (a most genial fellow) was only too delighted to have me,*
> *as all his hands are green and he wanted badly to have a man*
> *of experience. So it's a question of teaching the Navy how to sail,*
> *it seems. Hope I prove my use. Just giving my belly a good fill of*
> *breakfast on shore in preparation. Love to all the family. C*

It was a very easy sail to the Hook, which was just as well for our naval crew, mainly consisting of clerks from the Chatham base, who had never been to sea before, let alone in a yacht. I was in charge of one watch, the skipper the other. We didn't have to tack once during one leg down to Ostend, and then to the Hook. We anchored off Rotterdam Yacht Club. The navy rowed me ashore, wearing my bowler hat and waving my brolly aloft, ready for the wedding. I reached Brussels by train to join up with John and Mervyn, in time to celebrate a stag night on the eve of the church ceremony next day. John was in limbo having had the civil wedding in the mairie that morning. I joined the large family party staying in a hotel that Montgomery had made his Brussels headquarters. The reception took place there. It was a good party with memorable speeches from uncles, and of course the bride looking radiant. I paid my passage home.

It was August and Cowes Week, and John Bunting and I crewed in a very enjoyable Round the Isle race. The sun shone. It took nearly 24 hours for the owners to gain their mug for finishing. Just short of the line the wind dropped, the tide turned against us, so we had to anchor and wait for it to change the next morning. Again, as had happened to me before, jostling at the start we split the spinnaker. But the genial young couple who owned the yacht made no bones about it.

John, Mervyn and I had previously made ourselves at home on the Solent on many occasions sailing twelve-foot dinghies, based at Wootton Creak. Following my old sea scout master, from Ampleforth, Fr. Jerome, we stayed in the outbuildings belonging to two tough old spinster sisters, the Dorrien-Smiths, living in a cottage on the shore. They had been brought up on Tresco on the Scilly Isles, leased by their family from the Duchy of Cornwall. They went round smoking pipes. They were artists and had the walls of their cottage covered in their paintings, also photos of the Scilly Isles, mostly of offshore wrecks. We sailed their dinghies carefree, as the young scouts before us. There was no question of escort vessels, life jackets or buoyancy, as we sailed over to Portsmouth or up the Beaulieu River to Buckler's Hard.

John, Mervyn and I had also paid a visit to the Isle of Wight in midwinter. Being in a state of shock the day the news broke that the King had suddenly died, and with rugger the next day cancelled, I phoned them both up, and one other, suggesting a trip to Wootton Creak. The four of us took the train down to catch the last ferry across to Ryde. There we took a taxi to drop us off at the entrance to the drive of Quarr Abbey, which adjoined the Creek. As related in my school days, I had stayed there before with Fr Jerome in the war on a sailing trip from the mainland. Just after midnight we found a huge haystack, roofed over, but open to the elements all round. We climbed up into it and buried ourselves in the hay. It was early February and cold. A monk discovering us at daybreak, very cross not a bit hospitable, asked us how we had the cheek to be there. Mervyn remembers that I was then ordered to carry a cross in a procession, with, as he said, bits of hay in my hair. Was this a penance? We made our way across the fields to the Dorrien-Smiths hoping for a better reception. They were their usual friendly selves, but just asked us to give notice when we wanted to drop in next time. We took a bus to the Needles at the far corner of the island. Filling our lungs with lots of fresh air we began to feel better about the recent sad news. We slept that night in more sheltered, if not luxurious conditions, in the good ladies' boat shed.

Autumn came, then winter and the dawn of a new year, 1952. It was my moment of truth, the year of my finals. I dropped all other activities, apart from Saturday rugby and the occasional party, as I concentrated on my studies. It was going to be first time this time. I was enjoying both the academic study and the direct contact of patients in the wards or out-patients. In March I had to take the first part of finals, the Pathology exam. This went quite well, so that was out of the way. The final hurdle was in November.

I took one long weekend off in August to join John Bunting, where he was on holiday with his family near Lymington on the Solent. They had a small cabin cruiser sailing yacht on hire for their stay. John and I sailed off in it, crossing in a gentle breeze towards Cowes. It was a heavenly evening, and John and myself, as was our wont, discussed deeply about our love of various authors. Graham Greene, Evelyn Waugh and George Orwell were some of our favourites. We sailed on to anchor for the night at our old haunt, Wootton Creek. It was getting busier now with the car ferry from Portsmouth. The two lady seadogs were still there. We sailed back to Lymington to be told off by John's father for selfishly taking the family boat away for so long. (Poor John was frequently put down by his father). It was a good break.

In November came the great moment for sitting finals. If all went well, I would be a doctor. Feeling on top of much of the numerous subjects to be tested in, I was reasonably confident. Having had extra tuition in Gynaecology from George Livingston, a registrar, I felt especially good at that. (George was later to turn up at Walberswick at his holiday house there). The written exams in all the subjects – Surgery, Medicine, Gynae, Orthopaedics – took place in a hall near the Albert Hall. Feeling low and pessimistic after my first paper, I called on John Bunting at Art School round the corner for some consolation. But other exams seemed to go better.

It's nice to have that good feeling when your brain is full of knowledge on a subject, writing it down. John very kindly presented me with a small silver crucifix he had fashioned himself when he heard I had qualified. I still have it. Was it to signify my agony but ultimate triumph?

The vivas were a different matter, with everything depending on them. Being confronted with an unknown patient, taking a history, then making out what is wrong with him or her from all the clues in your examination, a consultant awaiting your conclusion at the end of half an hour, in the atmosphere of an examination, is all very daunting. A stethoscope in your ear, what is the meaning of those sounds? Trembling hands palpating, patellar hammer tapping, what does it all mean? My medical viva was at UCH. My examiner showed me to a male patient on a couch behind curtains and left me to it. Hardly was he out of sight, when the patient sat up and whispered, "Liver on the right, spleen on the left – Banti's syndrome." He was obviously an old hand, brought out especially to confront the aspiring doctors. I was over the moon. I made an examination, found it as he said. But it rather overshadowed making any other observations. The examiner returned. His first question – what were the heart sounds? I was flummoxed. I hazarded a guess – normal. He didn't look too convinced. A few more inconsequential questions. Time was beginning to run out. He wasn't asking me for my hoped-for trump card. In desperation I managed to get out, "I did find an enlarged liver and spleen." Then, as if I had given long thought to it: "Well, it could be Banti's syndrome, sir." Was he already aware of the old-timer? I feared the worst.

However, other vivas went well. The ordeal was over, and one just had to now wait anxiously for the result.

The big moment – the list went up and I was on it. What a relief and joy! A doctor at last and MBBS after my name. It was all over after seven long but eventful and happy years. There were big celebrations that night.

From all my own experiences of going through the emotional turmoil of all these student years from being an adolescent to an adult, what general advice can I give to the young? Live life to the full. Never miss any good opportunity however daunting. You only go down that road once. Choose a partner for life with both your head and your heart. The theory that it is better to live together before marriage is not borne out by the facts. The divorce rate has never been higher. There is an excitement and fulfilment for two people in their life together, discovering and exploring uniquely for the first time something which previously has been forbidden fruit. It's akin to not spoiling Christmas by not having presents beforehand. My opinion is that it is better to have some rules and boundaries. You can have a lot of fun without any anxiety or regrets. You know where you are. Am I crying in the wind? Sex constantly thrown at you visually on the media, with heaving bodies, may revolt some. To others it may seem the norm to be copied in all circumstances. As the celibate monk so succinctly put it at my school leaving talk, the marriage act is something beautiful, God given, to be enjoyed, but always mindful that its *raison d'être* is procreation. A difficult act to follow, I know, but worth it and religious belief helps.

So what now did the future as a medical man hold in store for me?

# PART THREE
# QUALIFIED DOCTOR

# Newly Qualified

It was always the hope of everyone who qualified to get a house job in their own hospital. I was lucky enough to be posted with the Middlesex Hospital gastroenterologist Dr Hadley. It was an immediate transformation to be a doctor in charge of your own ward. The old saying was "Where do the medical students go and where do the doctors come from?"

A friend was on holiday for a week in the summer, so I took over his place as a House Surgeon at the Richmond Hospital. This gave me some confidence to start. With a registrar present in the day, a consultant doing a round once or twice a week, you were otherwise alone to take continuous care of male and female patients in two wards, by day and at night and weekends. In theory you could call on your registrar (mine lived in Chelsea) but you were loath to do so. There was a resident medical officer to call on but again you felt you must do your own thing. Little did patients realise that coming, as they thought, to a top teaching hospital, they could be looked after by a doctor qualified perhaps just one day.

Except by making a special arrangement, once started you never left the hospital in the whole of the six months. The only time I made use of this was when I wanted to play rugby for the hospital on a Saturday, and for Sunday lunch on occasions at home. You were entitled to a two-week holiday.

Remuneration was at the princely sum of £200 per year with board and lodge free. I am sure at that time the amount of pay didn't enter into the consideration of young doctors. The excitement, experience and especially the kudos of obtaining a post in your own teaching hospital was all that mattered. How changed is the outlook of young doctors actually going on strike over pay and conditions in recent years.

I was to immediately have my baptism of fire within a week of starting. It was the great London smog that killed hundreds if not thousands. In the middle of Soho, we were inundated with patients. Beds became short and others had to be utilised over in the surgical wards. Victims would come in extremely breathless and cyanosed. Several of my patients died. One such was sadly a misdiagnosis. The reason, which seems incredible now, is there was only one ECG machine on the whole of our side of the hospital with five or so floors. It was not on my floor when a middle-aged man came to my ward in the night through the hospital casualty department. There he had been diagnosed by another junior houseman as having a heart attack, on account of his complaint of central chest pain. To relieve his pain without any means of confirming the diagnosis (a chest X Ray was not easily arranged at night), I gave him some morphine, the worst thing possible. He died in the night of an acute chest infection.

My consultant Dr Hadley as a gastroenterologist performed gastroscopies with a rigid instrument. It was akin to sword swallowing, much to the fear and discomfort of the patient, despite heavy sedation. Thank goodness for fibre-optic flexible endoscopes nowadays.

I was lucky enough to get appointed for my next six months as House Physician at the Royal Northern Hospital, downhill from Highgate, with four different consultants. I wanted to continue on the medical rather than surgical side as my ambition then was to specialise in medicine. I was able to broaden my experience with specialists in endocrinology, dermatology, neurology and chests. Also, on my ward, at the Middlesex, had been a cardiology consultant and joining in his rounds had given me an insight into this speciality to complete my medical education.

The endocrinologist at the Northern was Professor Raymond Greene, brother of Graham the author. He had a special interest in the premenstrual syndrome, treating it with progesterone implants. My job was to insert this through a canula (a small tube) under the skin. Women always found this very distressing. I often wondered when they came for a second implant whether they claimed to be symptom free to avoid further treatment.

Cortisone tablets had just come available, but Professor Greene had in fact obtained the entire stock in the country for the Royal Northern Pharmacy. With the excitement of trying out a really new remedy, we used it on a man in shock from a myocardial infarction (heart attack). We were both amazed and delighted to see his condition immediately improve. We must have been the first to see this happen in British hospital practice.

1953 was before the arrival of steroid creams -eczema patients were never cured, coming back time after time for their repeat prescriptions of unpleasant tar ointments. For the chest physician I was employed at that time for the repeated need to re-inflate patients with an artificial pneu-mo-thorax to control their pulmonary TB. This entailed pumping air into the chest cavity to partly deflate the lung.

The Hospital being situated just up the road from the Holloway women's prison resulted in an inmate being admitted under my care. She was an elderly farmer's wife from Devon with a blood disorder. A particularly sweet person, we couldn't help feeling sorry for her, as, we understood, did half of Devon on her conviction. It was for arson, she having set fire to a nearby farmer's haystack. After living an impeccable life, it was done under extreme provocation. My being in touch with the prison medical officer led to an invitation to visit. Feeling rather exposed I was surprised that a young man walking around drew no attention.

Living conditions at the hospital were fairly primitive. I wonder how present-day doctors would have put up with it. Our sleeping quarters were in a line of cubicles under the roof in the attic. It quite put me back to my dormitory at school. However, doctors did dine separately from the rest of the staff in their own dining room, times being more class-conscious then.

Away from a teaching hospital, time off was more definitely arranged. I did get a half-day off in the week and every other weekend to get away. My first weekend on duty, I didn't slip away to church which I could have done by asking someone to cover for me. I thought this was a slippery slope of neglecting my religious obligations, so made the effort the next Sunday on duty. The nearest church was St Joseph's, halfway up Highgate Hill. There I was to meet the McDowell family, mother, son Michael and daughter Mary, little knowing she was to be my future wife. I am sure attending that Mass put me in good stead with my future mother-in-law. Michael and I often met at the same parties around Hampstead in the two years before Mary left school. When Mary started on the social scene Michael declared that there was only one person his sister was not to go out with, and it was me. I don't know how I deserved this. But its effect was probably only to intrigue Mary even more.

I bought my first personal car just prior to starting at the Northern – a Morris 8, again with a thermometer on its bonnet. I named it *Sue*. It proved a boon on my half day in Wimbledon fortnight to motor there through London and – unbelievable now – to park just outside the main gate.

I took the two weeks holiday I was entitled to in July and set off in Sue at the end of my Friday's work. I was joining my parents who had rented a tiny cottage just next to the Randolph Hotel in Reydon in Suffolk. It was getting dark as I was slowly making my way up the A12 and began to realise that my headlights were getting dimmer and dimmer. Luckily I made it just in time. It was to be my first visit to Southwold, to which Reydon adjoined, and I fell in love with it immediately.

Southwold in brilliant sunshine looked wonderful. Bathing in the sea near the harbour mouth, watching a gymkhana on the common, buying a pair of riding breeches for ten shillings at Mrs Critten's Red Cross stall in the marketplace and then using them with my father to ride at Jimmy Bugg's stable in Walberswick was all heaven. I did manage to throw in another taste of the sea in the middle of it by joining my old mate Peter Haward at Plymouth to take a yacht that had taken part in the Fastnet race from there back to the Hamble on the Solent.

I was still due to do my two-year National Service. But I managed to delay it by doing another six months, this time back at my old hospital the Middlesex as medical officer in the casualty department. It was lovely to be back. I could play again for the rugby 1st XV. It was also a great relief to be working a 9-5 day with every weekend free. In the six months of the job I can't remember being hassled at any time, all rather different from reports of A and E departments in recent times. Perhaps this was a result of a superabundance of hospitals in central London then as well as GPs being more accessible.

It was here that I was to meet the light of my life again, my future wife Mary. Her mother Kate thinking she had a chicken bone in her throat came to see an ENT specialist at the Middlesex Hospital. Bringing Mary with her and knowing I was working in the casualty she popped in to see me on her way. Mary visited her when she was later admitted for an oesophagoscopy, and came in to see me in my office. (No chicken bone was in fact was found.) It being the end of my day, I was able to accompany her to her mother and then straight on to the student pub adjoining the hospital, the One Tun for a drink. From there we proceeded to Billy Graham's evangelical mission being held at the Tottenham Football Stadium. Mary was driving her father's large limousine after a day at the races. After being thoroughly roused by Billy Graham, Mary drove me home for our first kiss. We never looked back.

Our courtship was short and sweet. Within two weeks of our first meeting Mary invited me to a dance at the Grosvenor Hotel in Park Lane with her family. I had been hesitating how to make that next move. The dance consolidated our relationship. We then met as often as possible. On one occasion, stepping out of our transport, Sue, in Leicester Square for the cinema, the Evening Standard being sold in front of us showed in big headlines on the back page: "Hopkins to play for Rosslyn Park". That certainly helped my efforts. Mary's parents came with her to the match against the Metropolitan Police. I didn't think I shone but didn't disgrace myself. It was after a fortnight's skiing at Obergurgl in April, previously arranged with a fellow medic, that I proposed. My doubting friends all said it was only my tan that made Mary accept.

## Marriage

We were married at the end of July 1954 after I had finished my casualty job and before I was due to be called up in August. Just prior to the wedding Mary's parents presented us with a baby Austin car, perhaps portents of things to come. I sold Sue but it had done valiant service taking us around in our courtship. Having a hole in the floor on the passenger side did cause a few problems with Mary's evening dress on the occasions she was wearing one. We married at St James' Spanish Place. Curly Kirwan was my best man. He made a noble substitute for my otherwise best friends Michael Hardy and Mervyn Shipsey. Both were away serving their country, the former fighting in Korea, the other stationed in Malaya. Curly had been both at Ampleforth and the Middlesex with me. The day before the wedding Curly and I, rather like Drake playing bowls before fighting the Armada, went to play cricket for the Old Amplefordians. Fortunately it rained all afternoon. Ensconced in the pavilion Curly and I at this very last moment took the opportunity to make up our speeches for the next day.

We had our honeymoon in France and Northern Spain, finishing up with the McDowell family at Thorpeness. Passing through passport control at Gatwick airport on our way to Le Touquet the official recognised Mary from her photo on the front of the Evening Standard and repeated the caption underneath: "The bride in the breeze.. The bridesmaids and ushers celebrated that evening at Hatchett's in Piccadilly, enjoying themselves so much the Hatchett owners asked what the party was celebrating. On being told, Mary and I were given a free evening there on our return.

## Call up in the RAMC

One week later I had to report at Camberley to join the Army in the RAMC. My best man Curly was joining up with me. We met at the One Tun and with Mary all three of us motored down together. The introduction was to stay in barracks for two weeks and be drilled by a sergeant major by day to put some shape into us. I wasn't going to lose my bride so soon, so arranged to stay with my old school friend Owen Heape, also in the RAMC and living nearby, while at the barracks Curly ruffled my bunk and called my name at roll call. We were given our uniform and booted up. It was to be the only time I wore my boots. The sergeant yelled at us, telling us off individually, but always ending up with "Sir". We were starting as lieutenants, not even second lieutenants. At one time being stood to attention and thinking I was doing rather well, the inspecting sergeant as he came up the line stopped at me and shouted, "Are you pregnant – Sir?" I immediately pulled in my stomach.

I was posted to Germany to the British Military Hospital at Rinteln on the Weser, just 20 minutes or so from the Pied Piper town of Hamelin. Having done 18 months in medical work I was able to be graded as a junior specialist in medicine and work in a hospital with all the extra experience this would give me, rather than as a regimental medical officer with troops.

To the envy of the other service wives, whose husbands had taken six months or more to arrange accommodation for them (the Army didn't automatically arrange it for National Service men), I found a comfortable boarding house for Mary and myself within two weeks.

We enjoyed our two years in Germany, one year at Rinteln and our last year at BMH Hamburg. I was the sole medical officer in this second posting, so anyone needing hospital medical care between the Baltic and the Dutch border and halfway to Hanover was my responsibility. I learnt a lot and despite my junior status I don't think anything went wrong. I had to laugh when later at Southwold the matron queried whether I should be pronouncing on chest X Rays myself. I thought of the hundred or so I had had to report on in my service time.

The Army was still in the position of the Occupying Force in Germany in 1954 when we first arrived. Many properties were still commandeered. In this way Mary and I spent many an enjoyable evening at the Officers' Club in a splendid building at Bückeburg near Rinteln. A hotel was still in use in our first winter, a short train journey away, where we stayed to ski and dinner dance. One of the ski runs on the ridge had the Russian zone on one side, so if you went off course one way, it landed you in a lot of trouble.

Situated in Germany I was able to indulge in two other sports that I loved, riding and sailing. A German cavalry regiment had been in existence in Hamelin with stables and an indoor riding arena. It was now available to us. Together with Queen Alexandra nurses from Rinteln BMH, Mary and I joined in the school, still run by its same German sergeant, to be bawled at by him from the centre of the ring. We later took our horses out to ride through the forests on the hills above the town. On one occasion with a married RASC officer stationed at Hamelin we ended up breathless at a restaurant after a long canter. Mary arrived after the two of us looking flushed and ravishing. I saw the look on the officer's face was the same as mine. There followed later an indecent proposal. I was too taken aback to be angry.

I had two short cruises in the Baltic from the Kiel Yacht club, one with a fellow officer up to the coast to spend a night in the first harbour inside Denmark. Mary came on another occasion to reach an inlet just up the coast. Tying up to a quayside and going ashore for a good meal at a restaurant, Mary, who had never really sailed before, said this was fun. She changed her mind on the return sail, when first we had a thunderstorm and then a flat calm. We arrived back at port very late. To get back on duty the next morning in time, Mary had to drive us the hundred miles or more through the night.

Times were changing. Within a few months of our arrival, we stopped being the occupying force. Germany was beginning to get back on its feet. The Kiel yacht club, we now used, consisted of a few sheds, the magnificent clubhouse in occupation when visiting in 1950 having been handed back. But there were still perks to be had. We could buy petrol at a special rate, as also alcohol – gin at one pound a bottle from the NAAFI. The autobahns were nearly empty to get around on. There was no purchase tax on buying a car if you kept it there for a year. I had hoped to do this on time selling the baby Austin back in England and buying a new Morris Minor. But one of the many London dock strikes of those days caused a month's delay, so I had to extend my national service by a month to avoid the tax. Travelling to Cologne to pick up the Morris I was horrified by the devastation of our bombing still existing – large numbers of blackened skeletal buildings. No wonder when I called on one house looking for lodging on first arriving, the man came to the door very angry, saying, "You bombed us!" However, this was the only time this happened. By contrast, when we arrived at the much bombed Hamburg all the bomb sites had been cleaned up.

The German rugger team in Hanover that I played against couldn't have been more friendly, singing as we passed the large jug of beer round in a circle. The last but one to finish the jug had to pay for it. Playing for the Hanover Garrison XV we had a fixture against the Berlin Garrison.

This meant travelling by train through the night with the blinds down. If you let them up, you could be shot at. Staying for the weekend Mary and I took the opportunity to visit the Russian zone of Berlin. We were told you could buy Meissen china cheaply there. Servicemen could go there as long as they wore uniform. With the underground train taking us through the border, some fellow passengers became very alarmed to see me. They tried to warn me that the next station would be the Russian zone. Walking the streets, we felt very conspicuous. The fierce looking police stood on every corner. We worried as we had left Frances our precious infant at the hotel... would we get back again? The shopkeeper refused to let us buy anything with the West German Mark at a special rate. We did come away with a very nice cut glass bowl, still in existence. It was a great relief to be back in the British zone and our hotel once again.

Frances had been born very happily at Rinteln BMH in August,1955, delivered by the good Colonel McNie. Mary's mother Kate came out to be with us. Being unused to cooking ,having had a cook in her house all her life, Mary going into labour in the late evening, she worried more through the night how she was going to cook the scrambled egg at break-fast, that I had asked for, than about her daughter.

The journey to Hamburg on my transfer there took place in early January in the depth of winter. We set off in our Morris Minor loaded with luggage and Frances in her carrycot on the back seat. Snow lay thick on the ground with the weather blizzarding most of the way. The country-side north from Hanover looked particularly bleak. There were few signs of habitation and barely a car passed us all day. Suddenly through the blinding snow a signpost appeared pointing off the road. It read Belsen. We felt we just had to see it. Just a mile or two off the road we came across it. There it was – large snow-covered mounds, with on each a small board, one such labelled *'hier ruhen 1000 tote' (Here lie 1000 dead.)* The silence was eerie. The forest seemed to be gradually taking over as if to hide the shame. We motored back to the main road and continued our journey with a great chill in our hearts. We finally passed through Luneberg Heath, equally desolate where Montgomery signed the surrender declaration ending the war, to at last arrive at Hamburg well after dark.

I was to be in demand that first night, my predecessor having fled on my arrival. A major's wife was admitted in the early hours with a suba-rachnoid haemorrhage. Tired as I was after a long journey, I performed the necessary lumbar puncture to confirm it, and made arrangements for her immediate transfer to England.

At Hamburg I developed a very happy relationship with my German counterparts. As to be related later, I visited the local hospital, to be intro-duced to their recent discovery of the oral treatment for diabetes. Mary and I became great friends with a local German surgeon who deputised when my opposite surgical number Major Duggan was on leave. An Austrian, interned when living in England at the outbreak of war, he invited us to see the opera, Die Fledermaus. An entertainment that we just had to take our visitors to was the notorious Reeperbahn where the Beatles later found success, and women wrestled in mud. One bit of drama happened just before we left. It was the beginning of the build up to Suez. A tank regi-ment was about to be shipped out to Cyprus from the Hamburg docks, when a tank man was admitted under my care as a suspected case of poli-omyelitis. A general had to await my diagnosis as to whether the regiment had to stay in quarantine or not. A lumbar puncture revealed a simple virus. I was able to give the all clear – the one moment of power in my life!

## Back in Blighty

On demob in September 1956, we returned to England to stay at Mary's lovely parental home in Highgate, Mary pregnant again. I was still wishing to specialise, a hope I am pleased never came about. I am sure I was a more suitable person for general practice, and very happy the way it came about. To fill in time while preparing to take the necessary Primary Fellowship exam I joined a general practice in Hendon as a trainee. I had been doing a correspondence course while in the Army and while a trainee attended any medical meeting possible. In this way I certainly built up my medi-cal knowledge. Taking the exam in the Spring of 1957 I passed the writ-ten but failed the practical. With Christina our second child's arrival in December it was really time to make my living as a GP.

My trainer was quite honest. Before I came, he said he learnt more from his trainees than anything he could do for them. But treating patients away from the hospital environment seems very strange and daunting at first, and takes a little time to get used to, so I was grateful for the nine months with Dr Livingstone. He did teach me one thing that I continued – having a supply of jelly babies in the surgery for children.

I wanted to get into a country practice where knowledge of obstetrics would be much needed. On second application I was taken on as the House Surgeon at the Maternity Unit at the Whittington Hospital just down the road from Highgate. It meant living in, but it had to be done. I wouldn't have reached Southwold without it. I was soon into all the complications of obstetrics, using forceps, dealing with breach presentations and twins as well as normal deliveries. I felt very confident at the end of the six months, when my final hurdle of finding a general practice had to be taken.

## Applying for a practice

Finding a practice in 1957 was quite different from now in the 21st Century. Whereas now pleasant country town practices sometimes don't even get one applicant, in 1957 I was competing against thirty or more others. I was ideally qualified, having done two six-month medical house jobs, six months in A&E, two years as a medical officer in British Military Hospitals, six months as a trainee GP and now in the last months of six months obstetrics. My one drawback I am sure was being a Catholic. Religious belief meant a lot more then. Married with two daughters aged one and two it was time to properly earn my living. Housed comfortably in the in-laws's large house in Highgate, at least we were not on the streets.

In those last months of 1957, I applied through the BMA to several practices and received interviews for just two. One was at rather dreary looking Thame, Oxfordshire; the other, where Heathrow now is. The form was to queue up with your wife (a wife was definitely an integral part of the practice) for a ten-minute slot. I am eternally grateful I failed both. Then a friend of my in-laws, a fellow RC wanting a partner in his practice at

– of all places – Kings Cross adjoined to the red-light district (he himself living in style in Hampstead), offered me the post. One compensation was that he looked after a number of convents and the Jesuits at Farm Street. Feeling desperate in my last weeks at the Whittington hospital, I accepted – my only chance.

Then on New Year's Eve, finishing my list in theatre on my very last day, Mary phoned me. The BMA had informed us that a partner was wanted for a practice at Southwold. I couldn't believe my luck. I had known Southwold from the holiday there four years before and regarded it as a gem on the East coast, as I described it to my obstetric registrar, a New Zealander. This is what I had really wanted – a country practice far from hospitals, where medicine could really be practised.

I managed to find Dr Peter Westall the senior partner on the phone. Somehow, we clicked. I think he liked my monastic school credentials from Ampleforth, as he had leanings himself to Catholicism, but above all he wanted my experience in obstetrics. He had had the bad luck, I found later, to lose a mother in labour. He immediately invited me to come down to stay a night at his home. My one ace (as I thought) actually failed. I knew though not closely Bruce Ogilvie was in practice in Southwold having been at medical school with me, so I mentioned to Peter that I knew him. (Bruce's cousin Stuart Ogilvie, owner of Thorpeness, and his wife had in fact attended our wedding). But on phoning Bruce after my call, Bruce denied any knowledge of me. However, on asking his wife Dizzy did she know anyone of my name, she said, "Didn't he marry Mary McDowell?" – the family being yearly visitors to Thorpeness. Bruce quickly phoned Peter back to say yes, he did vaguely remember me now, but he really knew my wife and she was lovely.

Picked up at Beccles by Peter's wife Peggy, she took me to their house and surgery at Stoven. As she busied herself with supper, and with Peter still at his surgery, I was left in the drawing room with their four lovely children aged six to twelve. We got on splendidly, joking and telling riddles. At the end they told their parents they must choose Dr Hopkins. My first interview had gone down well. Peter, a very affable person, entertained me at supper with wine – another easy interview. The other partner Graham

Bracewell came to see me after supper. It was a more sober affair... the first question was – what would I do about patients wanting contraception? I said if any problem I would refer a patient to him.

The next morning passing through the countryside, frosty and in brilliant sunshine, Peter took me to see Southwold and Mrs Mills, the wife of the doctor now dying of a brain tumour, whom they wanted replaced. They lived and practiced at 15 North Parade – a rather different part of Southwold from the part I had seen on my holiday. Peter showed me the Southwold Cottage Hospital with its fourteen or so beds, an operating theatre for minor ops and an X-Ray machine, operated by the matron. I was delighted. Peter explained that with three partners they operated in three areas; my part would be Southwold, Blythburgh and tributaries of the Blyth and Walberswick; himself inland from Wangford in the centre; and Graham, living and holding his surgery at his house at Wrentham, looked after the countryside around. All told, the practice took place in beautiful countryside with a charming country town, having the delight of being beside the sea. As Peter put me back on the train with excitement in my heart, he warned me that with thirty other applicants it was only fair that he gave some of them a formal interview.

Back in London I felt I had to warn the Kings Cross practice doctor of the possibility now of going to Suffolk. He phoned me shortly afterwards to say his wife thought I obviously wasn't keen on joining him so struck me off. I was in limbo, back to square one. I waited anxiously. The phone call came from Peter a few days later. He wanted me to join him in one week's time. Hurrah!

# PART FOUR
# SOUTHWOLD
# GENERAL PRACTICE

# Settling in

I was to start work on a Wednesday morning, this being my half day. Travelling down on my own the evening before I arrived to stay with Mrs Mills. Nothing else had been arranged. I slept in her cold attic, waking next morning to find Southwold in a fog. I was told this never happened there. North Parade looked particularly gloomy. With a sinking feeling in my stomach and the daunting prospect of facing my first patients, Mrs Mills produced a bloater for my breakfast. I turned it down.

The patients arrived. There was no appointment system and no assistants of any sort. I did my first calls. I was feeling as low in spirits as the gloom of the day, wondering now what I had brought my young family to, away from our family and friends in London with nowhere to stay. Mary arrived by train at Halesworth in the afternoon looking so bright and cheerful, no doubt at the prospect of coming to a place I had cracked up so much. As we went under the bridge to leave the station, I felt tears coming down my cheeks. We all slept in the freezing attic that night. Clever Mary next morning quickly fixed us all up through Adnam's Estate Agent to rent the "cottage" on South Green that same day. Things immediately began to look up, as did the weather two weeks later.

Southwold certainly then had an old-fashioned charm. At that time there were many of its characters around – the old fishermen, families that had lived in Southwold for generations, a smaller proportion of retired and second homes. I particularly liked two elderly spinster sisters who had lived all their life in a house in Victoria Street who called themselves Old Victorians. Southwold was not on the map then and I had to describe it to Londoners as being somewhere between Lowestoft and Aldeburgh known for its Festival.

Very often during those first summers, porpoises could be seen just out to sea. They seemed to be following us along the beach. Regularly once a week at that time a Thames Barge could still be seen passing by in full sail, carrying its cargo along the coast to and from Great Yarmouth. In the town were three butchers, two more pubs than now, five garages, three selling petrol, and three cobblers, all manned by locals. One of the cobblers, Jack Farrington, a patient of mine, was the first violinist in the Southwold orchestra. He also played the fiddle at the Thorpeness Country Club Saturday evening dances. It was said he played the violin better than he mended shoes.

Another patient, old Sam Watson, and his mate were still fishing for herring in October. Rowing out from the shore just in front of us, they set out a drift net for an hour or so. Hauling it in they returned to the beach with a large catch, for us to dash down with a bucket and pay sixpence for a fill. Also, as the nights began to draw in in the Autumn and the visitors left the beach, so the anglers began to line up with their rods, to catch the cod and bass, a row of lights shining as they continued to fish through the night.

The station building still stood there at Station Road as a relic of the old Southwold railway.

Also showing the scars of World War II in Southwold were the bomb-sites of the old Marlborough and Grand Hotels, not yet developed. Jack Denny was still making up suits in his shop in the marketplace. He made me two. One was of a good strong Harris Tweed that I chose as suitable for a country doctor. He admitted he had already used the cloth for someone else, but "You won't meet the person," he said. He was wrong. At a meet of the Waveney Harriers, there was Lady Somerleyton wearing the very same cloth.

At that time there were three more grocers in old-fashioned corner shops and a fourth in Victoria Street. The most fashionable, owned by George Bumpstead with its slicing bacon machine, featured in a Sunday paper magazine. Winny's in Victoria Street, run by the old lady of that name living above the shop, opened all hours. It was so useful when with a young family, finding yourself without supper at 8 o' clock, you could buy a tin of baked beans with sausage. The gasworks off Station road was still supplying the town. Every evening the lamplighter passed us along North Parade, touching up each gas lamp with a long pole. All this remains etched in my memory. To my mind, something I witnessed epitomised Southwold of that time. It occurred at the corner shop between East and Trinity Street. Sir George Lacon was shopping there. As he was leaving at the door a voice from the counter within shouted out, "Oh Sir George, Sir George, you've forgotten your green shield stamps."

My parish priest Canon McBride, soon after my arrival, mentioned two old Amplefordians living in the area, I am sure to make me feel at home. The first, Giles Foster, had been a friend at school, but I had lost touch. The name of the other, John Levett-Scrivener, gave an instant chill in the stomach. It was he, when head of the house, who had told me in the lunch break that he was going to beat me that night. It didn't happen, as related in my school days. Canon McBride went on to tell an interesting history about the Levett-Scrivener family. As the village squires of Sibton at the time of the Reformation, they had taken stone from the dissolved abbey to build themselves a house. It is still called 'The Abbey'. But as a result of this action there was said to be a curse on the family so that the first-born son never inherited the estate. But now that John's father had married a Chilean who was a Catholic, John was brought up as one and sent to Ampleforth. John did have a heart attack in his forties while his father was alive but did succeed to outlive him. The same has happened with the next generation. (I have to say on mentioning this story to John's wife Juliet after his death she denied it was true).

I was on probation for six months. Peter passed a lot of his work on to me. This meant two surgeries at Wangford, including Saturday, and branch surgeries twice a week at Blythburgh and Wenhaston. I also had to take over his 2–3 rounds a week at the Geriatric Hospital at Bulcamp. Even now 30 years after retirement I still have disturbed dreams of getting around in time. I was very conscious of the opposition of the other four doctors in the town. Being myself placed on North Parade and they in the High Street and South Green, I felt very much the poor relation. Typically, the lady at Stonehouse on Gun Hill was looked after by the High Street practice while I attended the maid. Outside in the country however, living on his estate, the practice did have on its books the Lord Lieutenant of the county, the Earl John Stradbroke. As a National Health patient he was quite happy to take his turn with everyone else in the waiting room.

My predecessor in the practice before Dr Mills had been Dr Collings; he and in particular his son Dennis are much mentioned in Ronald Binns' book about George Orwell's connection with Southwold. I had no idea about this when Dennis, his wife Eleanor and daughter Susan were patients of mine. Dennis was an eccentric character whose passion for collecting never ceased. Eleanor seemed the most ordinary of housewives. It came as quite a shock to discover in Ronald Binns' book she had once been a lover of Orwell before her marriage. He describes her in a letter as having "a nice white body". When I had to examine her daughter I also remember being struck by the whiteness of her body. Perhaps it was hereditary.

I gradually found my way round the practice. Mrs Aldred, who had the branch surgery in her cottage front room at Blythburgh, was obviously not sure of me at first. She didn't like change, the usual Suffolk reserve, and didn't at first give me the customary refreshment at the end of the 11 o'clock surgery. She soon thawed and at Christmas she supplied the most delicious mince pies. When I praised them, Christmas continued all year round! Her husband Bob rented a few fields around the village using his two Suffolk Punches. These greeted me out of their stable door on the side of the house as I arrived. On one memorable occasion on my rounds, passing Bob ploughing a field by the roadside, he invited me to put a hand to the plough – so I did a furrow.

Mrs Morris, who kept the branch surgery at her house in the middle of Blackheath Wenhaston, greeted me like a long-lost friend. Trying to find my way there the first time I couldn't believe the surgery existed down this long bramble-hedged track, and turned back. I was reassured by a villager it was correct. Patients stayed in the house, me in a shed in the garden connected by a long wire to ring a bell for the next patient. The examination couch was a double bed. The patients in the house couldn't see when the last one left. On one occasion feeling very tired after seeing a patient off

I felt I must have a rest on the bed. Soon asleep, I woke in panic wondering how long it had been. On ringing the bell, the next patient arrived looking at me a bit askance. Mrs Morris, in her seventies, told me her husband had been a well-digger. Sadly, she died some ten years later, and the surgery had to move elsewhere in the village.

One place visited on most days on my rounds was the Southwold Hospital. Looked after by Matron Noller and her staff of nurses, 24/7, it was such an asset to the practice. Its fourteen beds meant patients could be looked after for a variety of conditions not needing a major hospital, and more satisfactorily than at home. This included illnesses such as chest conditions, strokes (no major interventions then), post-operative and terminal care. There were physiotherapists at hand, later to have a full department of their own. The X-Ray machine, still functioning in my earlier days, was a great diagnostic aid. Perhaps best of all in my first twenty years or so, for myself and for the whole population both resident and on holiday, was the operating theatre and nurses on hand twenty-four hours a day to receive and deal in the first place with minor injuries and medical problems. It was a port of call anytime for anyone in need, so one of the local GPs could then be called in to deal with it. Those were blissful days for Southwold and all around, unlike now, everyone having to drive twenty miles to the James Paget and queue for perhaps hours in the A and E. For me it was satisfying to be able to do suturing and deal with minor injuries such as a dislocated shoulder in ideal conditions and feel like a real doctor. One summer in particular, swarms of jellyfish brought a large number of holiday makers to the hospital. Being paid almost as much for a temporary resident, who could take just a few minutes to see, I encouraged the hospital staff to send for me. A rumour was spread around that the doctors were letting off bags of jellyfish at the end of the pier. Some visitors, worried they were bothering me, I explained that my resident patients were my bread and butter, but they were my jam.

Country doctors were expected to do everything. With my zeal to be a complete doctor I am sure I did some things out of my orbit. One of these was to give anaesthetics, until the arrival of my partner David King-Davies qualified in this. The local dentists expected me to give gas and air when necessary. I had had just a little experience in this. My partner Graham Bracewell asked me to give the anaesthetic at Southwold Hospital to a young baby for a circumcision. All went well.

The Wangford surgery I attended twice a week would, I am sure, not meet the approval of the Health Authorities nowadays. Situated on its own in an outhouse where Graham's uncle must have practiced before, it was the subject of much disquiet by the villagers. It comprised a small waiting area and a consulting room. On the window shelf in the waiting area for patients to collect were left their repeat prescriptions – sleeping pills, tranquilisers, the lot. The door was never locked. The same arrangements were made at the Stoven and Wrentham surgeries. At both there was also just a door separating the waiting patients from the consultation going on the other side. Particularly with deaf patients being questioned, all ears were listening. Graham Bracewell was very proud of his chaise longue used as his examination couch at Wrentham, but not especially liked by his patients. Graham had to take over at short notice from his father on his sudden death without any general practice experience himself, so continued with several of his father's rather old-fashioned remedies. One remedy for stomach complaints was using his palm as a measure for a powder to add to a bottle of water. I had to continue prescribing the different coloured fluids that Graham said his patients swore by as 'tonics', as also a special mixture for colds. It was a hark-back to the penny practice.

Communication was a little more primitive in those days before mobiles. One method to get in touch when in the Blythburgh area was, like the removal firm Carter Patterson, for Mrs Aldred to put a cardboard square in her front window. This signalled me to stop and use her phone to contact home, or later the receptionists at the surgery. Until the latter came this meant someone had to be continuously on the phone at home to receive messages when I was out on call in the day or when on duty for the practice at night or weekends. This, in our early years, meant Mary had to be housebound or leave our daily in charge to take calls.

Our first daily, Greta, had just left school age fifteen when she took on this possibly vital role as well as doing the housework and taking some of the care of the children. She cycled to us the three miles from Wangford

*Mary entering St James's, Spanish Place for our wedding in July 1954.*

*Leaving the church after our wedding.*

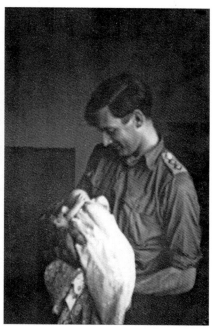

*Our first arrival, Frances, in my arms.
I was a Lieutenant in the RAMC.*

*Greta's wedding at Wangford Church.*
*Frances and Tina are bridesmaids ... James in the bow tie.*

*William and me, winners of the family tennis tournament.*
*Our fellow finalists were the two Johns, Hashim and Wheeler.*

*10 North Parade. Our first home and surgery.*

*Mrs Morris at the gate of her home and our branch Surgery in the shed behind her.*

*Frances and Tina in the Southwold Hospital float, processing through the town.*

*Calling on Southwold Hospital with Frances and Tina on Christmas Day 1960.*
*Matron Noller is top centre.*

*The town band passing 10 North Parade.*

*Carnival procession down Southwold High Street.*
*Me representing the town doctor 100 years previously.*

East Anglian Daily Times, Monday, December 5, 1988  Page 17

## PERSONALITY PIECE

Bob Aldred, and right, Bob before he retired, working the land with his horses in the shadow of Blythburgh Church. The bucket on the plough contained potatos for planting by hand — they were dropped one by one into the furrow.

# *Philosophy of a cheerful man*

**By Cathy Brown**

### 'It isn't any good getting riled, is it?'

"THERE are only two things you want in life — a bit of luck and good health. You can always get that shilling because there are 24 hours in the day and the night, and you can work 15 or 16 of them."

That is the philosophy of until shortly before he married Dorothy, at Blythburgh Church, in 1931.

"I stopped because I wanted to get a house."

Bob went into contract work with horses, and then into farming.

When they took over Lion House, on the main road gery — but since her death, Bob has carried on the tradition himself.

"He has continued to receive patients in his back parlour and allowed me the use of his front room as a surgery every Tuesday morning since," says Dr Christopher Hopkins.

"He has also continued the the house was owned by Leytons brewery in Yarmouth, and in the mid-50s the company decided to end the licence. Bob and Dorothy were offered a pub instead, but "I wasn't going to take a pub over," Bob says. And so he decided to try to buy the house.

He cycled to Wangford as most mainland ports.

"I wouldn't have been there if I hadn't been to sea."

Once he was farming, he didn't have time to travel at all.

"I forgot what Lowestoft was like. I never went til I packed in."

Bob and Dorothy had no nowadays relies on the buses to get about "unless I have friends to pick me up."

He has a lot of friends, and "the village treat me marvellous. There is always someone bringing me something."

Dr Hopkins remembers with pleasure how Bob's Suffolk Punches greeted him vision cameras, and passers by would stop their cars to take photographs of him and his horses.

On one occasion, he remembers, there were literally a dozen shutters clicking — and one man took the risk of lying in the furrow to frame a particularly artistic shot. But Bob's way of life was no romantic vision, just very hard work.

Even then he says, "I suppose fishing is nearly twice as

*Article in the EADT describing Bob Aldred's life and holding a branch Surgery.*
*(Reproduced by kind permission of the East Anglian Daily Times)*

---

## pulse|news

# Government signals plan to scrutinise use of deputising

**By Sarah Neville**

Senior Government officials have made clear to FPC administrators that they are expected to take a much closer look at GPs' use of deputising.

The tough new stance was spelled out during a top-level seminar on deputising organised by Nottinghamshire FPC and attended by around 80 senior FPC officials from almost 40 FPC's nationwide.

And it emerged during the seminar that the new deputising liaison officers are seen as the tool which the Government believes should be used to enforce it.

David Wilde, senior principal with the Department of Health's family practitioner services division, told the seminar that FPC deputising services sub-committees should regard liaison officers as an 'opportunity to improve their monitoring and control'.

While GPs needed time off, 'standards of services must be maintained and expenses falling on the taxpayer controlled'.

Some checks on use of the service must be made, given that the cost to the taxpayer of 12 visits per 1000 patients annually was $36 million, said Mr Wilde.

And, in what could prove a controversial suggestion among many GPs, the senior medical officer with the department, Dr David Bellamy, said the liaison officers 'could be involved in the selection of deputising doctors', taking into account the 'medical and linguistic abilities' of the applicants.

Leeds FPC chief executive Doug Allaway said it was clear that they were expected to keep much closer checks on the extent to which their doctors used deputising services.

The comments of the department officials had been underscored by the report of the Commons public accounts committee last month which said the Government was planning to issue 'more robust' advice on deputising and had suggested that payment of doctors who used the service might in future be dependent on the provision of full information about their use of deputising services.

Dr Christopher Hopkins with Bob Aldred – sweet treats are too good to keep for Christmas.

## Sweet Yuletide all year

Christmas lasts all year for GP Dr Christopher Hopkins.

And he can thank his branch surgery host, farmer Bob Aldred, for the sweet treat.

Dr Hopkins has been feasting on mince pies provided by his host every week for the past 30 of the 50 years he's held weekly surgery on the Aldred farm.

'They are absolutely delicious,' Dr Hopkins declared. 'But I am sure they are terribly bad for you.'

# *A COMPELLING FIRST CHOICE*

150

*With genuine*

## Patients happy with deputising services

The majority of patients are the service provided by Air

*Pulse article on the 50th anniverversary of holding a brach surgery at Bob Aldres's house.*

*The Aravind Children's Hospital, Tamil Nadu, India.*

*Visit to a temple after a camp. I have been garlanded by the priest.*

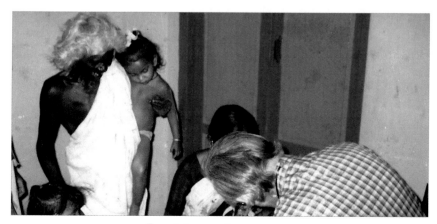

*Examining a patient at a camp.*

*Mary holding her play group at the Nutritional Centre.*

*Primary Health Centre Clinic, Vizhinjam, Kerala.*
*Note females queuing on one side, with males on the other.*

every morning including Sundays at first. She married quite young. Our daughters Frances and Tina were her bridesmaids at the Wangford church. Pregnancy followed, and I as her doctor delivered her personally at the GP maternity unit at the Patrick Stead Hospital, Halesworth.

A successor was needed. I looked around Blythburgh Hospital and selected the one I thought the most reliable and attractive – nursing assistant Carole. Asking Matron if we could have her to work for us, she gallantly said our need was greater than hers. Carole came to us for a number of years. The inevitable happened. She married, asked Frances and Tina to be bridesmaids at the Brampton church and I attended her pregnancy. I call this a wonderful picture of country practice.

Practices are now encouraged to amalgamate into larger and larger units. Single-handed doctors are positively discouraged, much to the loss of that close doctor-patient relationship. This was satisfying for the doctor, producing a father feeling – much frowned upon now – so that as with your own crying child you were happy to look after the most difficult of patients. With a relatively small list of around 1400 patients, I was kept on my toes not to lose any to other doctors. This competition between practices was certainly good from the patient's point of view. With the practice spreading over 100 square miles, and on call two nights a week and every third weekend, with many branch surgeries to fit in during the day, I was in fact worked hard. The evening surgery never started before 5.30pm and frequently went on after 7.00pm. There wasn't time to do all the visits to start the evening surgery any earlier. It made a long day.

I made a point in my early months of calling on every patient to introduce myself. One way this happened was literally to bump into one. Not long after my arrival, turning a corner into Marlborough Road in the dark from one emergency to another, I didn't see the light on an old fisherman's bicycle as he was wobbling his way back from the pub. As he landed on my bonnet and fell into the road, I asked him who was his doctor. "The gentleman on North Parade," he said. I said, "That's me." Taking him to the hospital, the X-Ray showed a fracture of the neck of femur so off to Lowestoft hospital he went. I was had up for dangerous driving. Doctor Borham, my rival, the magistrate at Southwold court, fined me £10, probably the least possible. The old fisherman was compensated with £2000 – good beer money – and a new hip to replace his old arthritic one.

A call to a patient in Blythburgh resulted in introducing myself to half the village. I was asked to see a 'Lady Kett' there, but no address was given. Assuming this meant a titled lady, I thought this would be no problem. But on asking at the first house I was told there was no such person and Kett was the commonest name in the village. The result – a series of Mrs Ketts had to be called on before finding the wizened old lady in Church Lane. She turned out to have a number of old remedies (or spells) herself, including that of keeping a pebble with a hole in it suspended under the bed for cramp.

Asked to judge the baby show at Wangford fete in my first summer, I felt this was a chance to ingratiate myself with the village mothers. Little did I realise there was only one mother I would make happy; all the others thought I was horrid.

July arrived. My probation was over, and I became a partner. I was not to have parity for ten years, such could senior partners keep the juniors down in those days. I remember a great feeling of elation; I had made it at last but we still had one thing missing – no fixed abode. In that first year we were to move seven times. Our rent of "The Cottage" on South Green finished at the end of May to make way for summer visitors. We found a house to rent in Marlborough Road just behind Mrs Mills. A telephone wire high above the road connected us to her phone so we could now take all the calls ourselves. Within a month we had to move again next door. This time we were next to a patient of mine, Mrs Cragie, who was soon to be the second oldest in Britain at 107. Born at Stoven six miles inland, she was told at the age of seven that she wouldn't survive if she didn't move to the sea. She came to Southwold and lived another 100 years. The oldest by six months lived at Lowestoft. Obviously, there must be something healthy about the East Coast. Graham gave us shelter for August and finally 10 North Parade came up for rent in September and subsequently for sale in January. We bought it for £2,500, houses there now going for over a million.

The good Mrs Williamson in Godyll Road came to our aid to bridge the gap of a night before one of our moves. Mary and the girls slept there while I went back again for a night in Mrs Mills' attic. She was now a widow, Dr Mills having died earlier in the summer at Southwold hospital. Mrs Williamson was the sister and aunt of two monks at Ampleforth, Frs Sebastian and Jerome, both mentioned in my school days. The world is indeed a small place. Jerome suddenly turned up one summer in a yacht at Southwold harbour. With him was Ralph May, my school explosives partner. I heard they made an abortive attempt to sail over to Holland but ran into trouble and had to turn back halfway.

We were to make our final move in 1972 to Ford House, Wangford, and have lived there at the time of writing for nearly 50 years. Its purchase was another fortuitous event in my life. Living in an attached Victorian house with no real garden, many of our friends and colleagues having quite grand houses and gardens, I had promised Mary if we hadn't found such by the time I was 45, I would move practice. I don't think in fact I had any real intention of doing this. Then aged 43 I was going down the Wangford High Street when I saw this rather dilapidated large Georgian type house with a field and garden behind. I knocked on the door and brazenly asked the lady who answered was it up for sale. She said, "Yes, it's on the market tomorrow." The price with its 3.5 acres was £9,500. Only using a remote agent in Woodbridge, just one other person came to see it. After nearly losing it by offering a ridiculously low price, the other buyer offering £9,000 was accepted, but then chance came back to me and I made it. It has been a marvellous family home since, associated with six weddings and a funeral, this last being my dear maiden aunt of 98, now buried in the churchyard. Since writing this sadly another funeral has occurred that of my dear wife Mary. She is now buried just over the wall that I built nearly 50 years ago.

I was to find the house had quite an interesting history. The Honourable Agnes Eden had owned it early in the century. Her nephew Anthony Eden, later to become our Prime Minister, came to stay frequently. One of the photos of a bygone age on show in the parish church showed a row of boys on the bank of the river Wang, dammed then for swimming, with a caption underneath 'A. Eden', dated 1906. There is a plaque under an oak tree on East Green Southwold that reads – *This oak tree was grown from an acorn procured by the Hon Miss Eden from the battlefield of Verdun and presented to the town in 1924.* It is said the Honourable Agnes made herself the grand lady of the village, putting herself above the Countess of Stradbroke. Girls in the village were made to curtsy to her. She had a parrot on show in front of the house and bred turkeys in the field as presents for friends at Christmas. The largest tombstone in the churchyard sited alongside the garden marks her grave. Also resident at Ford House before, during and after World War II was the Wangford village doctor, Dr Wight. He held his surgery in the house with the waiting patients huddled in the tiny room on the side of the house, just a door separating them from the consulting room.

I cannot claim to be much of a DIY man, but I am rather pleased at two of my achievements at Ford House. The first, with the assistance of Patrick Purves, just out of my Alma Mater, was replacing a rusty old corrugated iron roof on an adjacent outbuilding, with pantiles fortuitously lying about in the garden. The roofing withstood the epic storm of 1987 with not a pantile lost. My other boast is my Churchillian task of building a wall. I didn't like the look of fresh tombstones in the churchyard getting closer to one side of the garden. Again, there were many bricks left lying around from the wall next to the road being taken down and replaced to widen it. I made the wall one brick length thick so as not to worry if I went off-line. Taking a week off to hasten the job, I didn't realise how tough a labouring job could be. The first two days went well but getting up on the third morning I had had it, my muscles completely gone. But at a slower tempo the wall was eventually completed, and the living stay separated from the dead.

## Obstetrics

It was not long before my ability in obstetrics was called into action. Before the end of my first year Peter sent for me in the middle of the night to a home delivery, the mother then being delayed in her second stage of labour. I arrived with my forceps and without any bother brought the baby into the world. Such was Peter's relief and admiration that we were invited to dinner a few nights later. Within the next year or so I was to do three more forceps deliveries. One, at the Patrick Stead Maternity Unit, impressed the previously doubting Matron with my calmness. The two others were at home. One of the mothers was left rather long in the second stage. A difficult delivery requiring two episiotomies sadly resulted in a still-born baby. The other happened on my weekend off, but I always attended my own patients. Starting her labour weakly on the Saturday morning, I managed to go shooting all afternoon before being called by the midwife in the evening for a delayed second stage. The baby delivered, all of 10lb, I was to come across again as a sturdy Suffolk man on a shoot 40 years later. Starting off in our trailer reading the list of guns not knowing most of them I saw the name and recalled that delivery. I asked my neighbour if he knew Stephen Tonks. It was him.

Apart from these moments of intervention I had many happy normal deliveries both at the Patrick Stead and at home. One such memorable occasion was on a Sunday morning in Wangford, with a black cat asleep on the other side of the double bed. An easy delivery and then the joy of a little sister coming into the room to see her baby brother. One other for Jane, Jim Prior's wife, took place at her home in the Old Hall, Brampton. We had been chatting downstairs when she suddenly said things were happening. Rushing upstairs, my main concern being to tell Jim to get out of the room, as it was not then usual for husbands to be present, I delivered Sarah Jane safely into the world. She popped out one moment, a shout to Jim outside the door – "It's a girl!" – and the next moment he had popped the champagne bottle. A follow up happened years later at the reception held at the house for Jim's funeral. Chatting with Sarah Jane's husband, whom I had never met before, he asked me if I had ever met his wife. I had to say I was the first to lay my hands on her naked body upstairs. In retirement I am often amused by the shocked look on people's faces when I state "I have been responsible for a lot of babies round here you know".

After feeling so confident straight from my obstetric job, the years went by without the need of using forceps. It needs constant practice to keep one's hand in, so I began to feel I was that occasional obstetrician so frowned upon. I felt I had to support the campaign to stop the closure of the maternity unit at the Patrick Stead in the 90s, and even spoke at a meeting for this. I gathered applause when I said I would be happy to pay more taxes in aid of it, but felt some sense of relief though sadness when it happened.

## Unmarried Mothers

Unlike later in the century, up to the early sixties it was regarded as a great shame to be an unmarried mother. I was to see three single young girls hide the fact of pregnancies and arrange to have their confinement far away. Two were to have them immediately adopted; the third to make out that her own mother was the mother. Sadly, it was a psychological disaster for the boy. One of the girls, I heard about from her mother years later. When the law made it easier to discover their lost child, this did in fact enable her to meet up, to the great joy of both.

I also had a patient adopted and brought up in poor circumstances by a working-class couple. In middle age she became determined to find her mother. She did succeed with the help of the vicar, to discover that the family she had been taken from were rich and middle class. Her mother had had her adopted when in her forties, having a large family already. Visiting her mother, she found she had just suffered a severe stroke. She felt her mother realised who she was, but neither said anything. Meeting her siblings, she was warmly embraced by them all as their long-lost sister.

## Accidents

Accidents and emergencies were dealt with by the GPs themselves until towards the end of the millennium. There were no paramedics. The patient's doctor was generally to be called first and then the ambulance second. In the 60s, East Anglia developed a special GP service to be on call for road accidents. Unless out of hours, emergencies could cause great disruption to the round and especially during surgery hours. I was to be called to numerous road accidents in my time. Rain after a spell of dry weather often led me to expect one. Driving round now I am reminded of incidents on so many roads. The worst accident I remember happened on a Sunday morning. I was on call while sitting in church on the front right pew, so if necessary I could hear the telephone in the presbytery. No mobiles then so Mary had to attend Mass at a different time so she could answer the phone. A terrible wind was rattling the church windows when Mary rang. I was wanted for an accident on the A12 at Foals Watering. A lorry had jack-knifed and crushed a car going in the opposite direction. On arrival, there were already three bodies laid out on the verge with somehow more pathetically a dog at the end. The driver was dead crushed behind the wheel.

## Contact with the Law

Breathalyzers were not in existence in my early days. It was the local GP who had to make the decision. It happened that I was called one evening to the Southwold police station in place of the official police doctor, Doctor Borham. It was said he was not in a fit state himself. The man accused of drunken driving was a real son-of-the-soil Suffolk man. I performed the usual tests – finger/nose drill, walking in a straight line and observing for bloodshot eyes and dilated pupils. His wobbly gait left me in no doubt about his drunken state, and I had to pronounce him so. I heard he then used his pony and trap for getting about. Afterwards he bore me no ill will, greeting me when I met him at a pub with a friendly "Hello Doctor. Do have a pint."

I had a brush with the police myself, being overtaken and stopped by a police car inside the 30 mile limit at Aldeburgh. Mary and I were on our way to celebrate our wedding anniversary and no doubt I had had a G & T or two before we left home. It was fortunate I had taken the local police First Aid examination the week before. The Officer demanded my driving licence, looked at it and then said, "Oh I can't do anything doctor. You passed me in my First Aid test." They were all very hopeless at First Aid, but I had had to fail one who was even more hopeless than the rest. Luckily it wasn't him.

## Home Visits

The months and years rolled by. I came to know and become friendly with more and more in my care. One felt more and more part of one's patients' joys and sorrows. There is a saying: 'Make a doctor your friend but never a friend your doctor.' The latter case can cause embarrassment for some, but I found with some of my closest friends it could form a special bond. Paying frequent home visits, you came to know the whole family better. If I meet any of my old patients now, I remember them best when I ask where they lived.

Living close to many of my patients (Southwold was still inhabited by a larger number of permanent family residents) I was able to give some extra treatment. One such in Fieldstile Road was to a baby born at the same time as one of ours, so I regarded them as twins. Giving my own their infant injections when they were asleep, I did the same for the other. Another couple on St James Green had been unable to conceive after several years of marriage. Having heard it helped, I arranged for the husband to use a condom at the right time of the wife's cycle and then send for me to inject the contents into the cervical canal. No luck after 2–3 cycles. A year later however she did conceive, had three children in quick succession and then asked for the pill.

It was usual then to pay social calls on the elderly, if they were housebound, every 1–2 months or so. It was quite the custom for the more well-off to offer the doctor a glass of sherry. My opposite numbers in Southwold, Drs John Borham and Mary Leedham-Green, were said to reek of it. For me one such port of call was with a Colonel's widow in Blythburgh. A large glass was filled for me and I was told on finishing, it must have a pair of wings, so I had to have a second. I made a point of this being my last call in the morning. Lunch afterwards with Matron Emma Last at Blythburgh Hospital was always a merry affair.

## Sadness

Practice can never be without its sad moments. It was always my fear that I would have to attend a child dying slowly of some fatal illness. It didn't happen, but sadly I had two sudden deaths. One occurred unexpectedly when a previously fit child developed what seemed to the mother an ordinary cough one evening. She asked to come and fetch an antibiotic but didn't request a visit. It was a rare staphylococcal pneumonia, sadly, and he didn't survive the night.

Not long after I had another but not entirely unexpected death. The child had been attending a cardiologist for a cardiac arrhythmia causing occasional loss of consciousness. While running to catch her pony another attack happened. I was immediately called but sadly, despite desperately doing CPR all the way in the ambulance to Lowestoft Hospital, still functioning then, she didn't survive. The parents very kindly made me sit with them at the church funeral to make sure no one felt they had any ill feelings.

Tragedy was to strike a family of eleven children in Walberswick. Called by the mother to see two of her children unwell I arrived to find them gasping for breath. It was obvious air hunger. Asking the mother if they had taken anything, she said yes two days before she had found her 6-year-old feeding herself and her two year old brother aspirins from a bottle she had taken from high up on the dresser. Not realising the delayed affect, as they seemed all right then, she didn't worry. Sadly, nothing later could save them, and they died in Ipswich Hospital.

## Diagnosis

Diagnosis is the most important thing that a GP does. He is at the cutting edge. He being the first person a patient sees, making the right diagnosis can be a matter of life or death. Delay in the diagnosis of a cancer can have fatal results. Early diagnosis is now to the forefront again. A special breathalyser to detect early cancer is now on the cards to be used in doctor's surgeries. All this is wonderful, but the chief delay is still the patient coming to the doctor in the first place. That close doctor-patient relationship, so vital to prevent any inhibitions in approaching their doctors, has to some extent been lost, not to mention the barriers and time to get an appointment in the first place.

Diagnosis was one thing I felt most pleased and confident about. I often felt I hadn't given enough time to explain things to patients, but it was partly due to being deeply in thought about their diagnosis and what to do about it. One dictum I made to myself – *always do one more test than I thought necessary*. A family doctor can get all the credit. I often think of an old lady in my houseman days, having had an appendectomy, went on praising her doctor who sent her in rather than the clever surgeon who did the operation.

But what diagnoses or services in 32 years in my practice can I be most proud of? The most dramatic was an ectopic pregnancy. Called to a young woman alone in her house in bed complaining of a tummy pain, previously seen by two doctors and not diagnosed, I immediately realised what it was. I pressed I think gently on her abdomen when she immediately went unconscious. Alone with no mobile or telephone there, or in many houses in the Reydon council estate, I remembered one in a painter and decorator's house a few streets away. Luckily the wife was in. A phone call to Lowestoft Hospital for a doctor, blood and an ambulance had a rapid response. A drip was put up and then the patient was whisked away, to return recovered later. Another case was Falciparum Malaria. Having treated this in my military service in the RAMC (the intense headache having put me on the alert) the diagnosis of a sailor just returned after being sent ashore with appendicitis halfway up Africa was apparent. A blood test confirming the cause of his fever, he responded quickly to treatment for what can be a fatal disease.

One lady in her sixties came to me complaining of insomnia. I noticed her pallor. Confirming she was anaemic and then arranging a Barium enema X-Ray, although she had no bowel symptoms, resulted in a colonectomy for a malignant tumour. It was always so pleasing to see her about in her nineties.

Also satisfying was a man in his seventies coming to the surgery complaining of flu-like symptoms for two days. On hearing the murmur of mitral stenosis for the first time, I suspected sub-acute bacterial endocarditis, which proved correct on sending him into hospital.

After starting a Type 2 diabetic with oral treatment, I mentioned this to the Geriatric consultant from Ipswich while he paid his monthly visit to Southwold Hospital. He queried how could I as a GP have done this without reference to him? I replied saying I think I was in fact the first British doctor to use hypoglycaemics when medical officer at the British Military Hospital at Hamburg. Liaising with a German hospital when the drug had just been discovered in Germany, I was given bottles of the tablets. Using these on a sergeant just admitted to my ward with Type 2 Diabetes, I had the satisfaction of seeing him respond and therefore stay in the army as he didn't require insulin.

Three other diagnoses also gave me great satisfaction. One was an actinomycosis abscess on the neck. On first sending the patient to Ipswich with this diagnosis they didn't agree. On a second referral when the condition continued, they had to admit that I was right. For two other diagnoses I had the X-Ray machine at Southwold to help, one an atrial septal defect, the other an early case of pulmonary TB.

## Moving Premises

With the government paying for the building or renting of premises as well as receptionists and nurses in the early to mid-sixties, I was able to move my surgery out of my house. Our home was our own again. Perhaps our lovely golden retriever Dusty, lying at the top of the stairs and watching patients arrive at surgery times, missed them. He never barked unless they came out of hours.

Mary would have missed it in one way as at home she loved assisting me at my immunisation sessions. This included giving polio drops on sugar lumps to the infants. But our family was never entirely remote from the practice, as must be the case nowadays. Our son James, as a young teenager, was to discover this when he answered the phone to a young girl complaining about her periods. When he protested that he was only the doctor's son, she said, "Oh you must know, you are part of the family!"

Change of practice premises took place first next door and then, when local builder Biddy Denny invited me to Buckingham House in the High Street, I moved there. He had just bought it in quite hilarious circumstances. Applying for membership of the Blyth Club that had set itself up in the building for gentlemen of Southwold to play snooker and bridge, Denny was black-balled, not being of the professional class. Buying the premises over their heads, he then threw the club out. At the same time, he left the more 'establishment' medical practice in the High Street and joined the one north of the lighthouse, me. I was now in the centre of things. No longer did patients have to brave the biting east wind on North Parade. As a wag put it – the only patients east of me were drowning.

Having a receptionist now enabled me to have an appointment system. Thinking that having help in surgery administration meant I had more time for patients, I offered check-ups for patients in their forties, but very soon found that extra time didn't exist. I had to give it up. All my time was needed for dealing with patient's problems. This had priority. Some research suggests that check-ups for the healthy don't necessarily reduce morbidity. All this I was to argue at the time of my retirement. I did at least find time to send for and take the blood pressure of all my patients over forty.

## Religious Belief

What problems did I have being a Catholic doctor? In fact, prejudice against Catholics probably saved me from being accepted into some less favourable GP practices until Southwold came up at the right time. On my arrival the Southwold vicar immediately left my list but staying with me were a lovely retired Anglican Bishop and dear Canon Bonsey, retired Rector of Wrentham. I also seemed to take on a succession of non-conformist ministers as well as that of the Jehovah Witnesses.

The problem of contraception had to be dealt with. At first this wasn't very difficult as there was only the barrier method. If a woman wanted to be fitted with a cap, I would refer her to a clinic or a partner. But one woman left me after I refused to prescribe her condoms. But then in the mid-60s came the pill. Rather uneasily at first, I prescribed it only for married women. Early on an unmarried girl came to me. When I explained to her my difficulty with religious belief, she was so sweet. She quite understood: "It could condone immorality," she said. Soon I gave up and prescribed the pill for anyone of age.

Even more difficulty arose with the Abortion Act of 1967. I felt powerless, unable to advise anyone as my feelings were one-sided. I referred anyone requesting it to my partners. But when one of my women, after seeing Dr David King-Davies, told me he had persuaded her to keep the baby, I felt quite ashamed that I hadn't counselled her in the same way. Then a fifteen-year-old girl came to me with her mother, both very distressed. Having been assaulted by a family friend she had found herself pregnant. They didn't want to involve the police or anyone else. Feeling very sorry for them I phoned a gynaecologist I knew well, who saw her immediately. Like Pilate I felt I had washed my hands of her. But a few days later through the post came the form for a second doctor's signature. With a heavy heart and conscience, I signed it. I had to confess. But not wanting to go locally that Saturday on my way back from a hunt, passing by St Benet's church in Beccles at the right time, I had my chance. My horse Harlequin waited in his box as his master went inside to clear his soul.

I was mindful of the difference between now and before the Abortion Act of dealing with the situation. While a houseman at the Whittington in 1957, one of my almost daily jobs was to see girls, they were mostly young, in the casualty department with the after-effects of back street abortions. They were admitted and then put on my evening theatre list to clear up the debris. Once I was to recognise a nurse friend of my sister. We both made no mention of ever having seen each other before.

Church-going could have its hilarious moments. I was serving on the altar dressed in a white surplice when an elderly lady, Libby Purves's grand-mother, fainted at the back of the church. Summoned to her aid, as I stood over her she opened her eyes, looked up at me and said, "Am I in heaven?" The only time I have been taken for an angel.

I was to have another occasion of mistaken identity. Called to a part-ner's patient, unknown to me, an old lady in bed with a tummy pain, I asked her to lift up her nightie and examined her abdomen. Able to reas-sure her all was well, as I was leaving the room she called "Thank you, it was so nice of you to come and see me, VICAR."

Another time the laugh was on me. Having just recently heard a talk by a most zealous Catholic encouraging us to proselytize on every occasion, I was called to a lady unknown to me complaining of depression. When she told me she was a lapsed Catholic, I felt here was my opportunity of suggesting to her that certainly one person loved her – God – and re-join-ing a parish she would get a sense of companionship and support. After talking for a while, I began to realise she was nodding off. Feeling foolish when the penny dropped, I asked her if she had taken anything. She said yes, sleeping pills before I arrived. "Ambulance, quick!"

## Celebrations

One celebration that has taken place in Southwold every year since the Charter in 1489 is the Trinity Fair. This includes the Trinity luncheon with a number of speakers. I had attended several lunches without so to speak having to pay for it. Then in around my fifth year I had the dreaded call to give the speech on behalf of the professions. To my downfall, unaccustomed as I was to public speaking, I didn't prepare for it. After an initial few words I came to a full stop to the great embarrassment of all around, not least Mary. Eventually I managed to blurt out a few words about the need to safeguard Southwold Hospital against closure by being prepared to pay to privatise it. It was a warning some fifty years before it happened. I sat down to the greatest applause of the day, such was the company's relief it was over. I never made the mistake of not preparing a speech again, but the experience made the fear of public speaking even worse. But, as to be mentioned later, after taking up complementary medicine I managed to cure the phobia myself with 'the swish'.

One festive occasion I did really enjoy was to take part in a carnival procession through the streets of Southwold enacting the town of 100 years before. Dressed in a frock coat, top hat and carrying my black bag I represented the town's doctor of the time. Inside the bag I had put a bottle of 'good strong medicine'. Fortifying myself with this as we waited for the start in Pier Avenue then following the band up the High Street I was in the height of spirits. To the delight of the crowd lining the street I darted off the line at every opportunity to give every attractive lady I knew a big embrace.

Christmas was a special time for us in the practice. After our church service and before lunch we had a tour of the two hospitals. First to Southwold to have our first glass of cheer. Aged four and five, Frances and Tina were dressed up as nurses. A later year James came as a cowboy, shooting all the nurses; then to go on to Blythburgh Hospital where it was my duty to carve the turkey. More cheer and the chance of a kiss or two. A party of us had previously gone around the wards, singing all the old songs the elderly patients loved. In our first years the Swan at Southwold was particularly festive. Mary's parents staying there, we joined them for the dinner dances every evening. Bath Jones, the manager, dressed up as Father Christmas, distributing presents even to Mary and myself. The dances continued on New Year's Eve and Saturdays during the winter. One sight in Southwold that intrigued our children, not seen now, were the turkeys hanging upside down outside Baggots the butchers in Trinity Street. The two generations of Baggots were still alive. Both had been Mayors, the dear old man a patient of mine. One year in the week before Christmas all the Church choirs were invited to take turns to sing carols on the small green in front of the Post Office. Taking part, I say I was talent spotted by the leader of the Southwold Choral Society watching us. I was asked to join the choir for the Easter performance of the Messiah.

## Stormy Weather

Weather for a country practice could cause problems getting around. Three times it was snow and once the debris of the 1987 gale. In my first winter Walberswick became completely cut off by snow drifts. Anxious for a patient there, I asked my parents at home in London to send my skis by train to Halesworth. It was quite a disappointment when the thaw came too soon to take to them.

A sudden snow blizzard blocked the road back to Southwold while doing the morning surgery at Wangford. As a bus was turning around at the other side of a huge snowdrift near Reydon church, I managed to scramble through the snow just in time to catch a lift back to Southwold for my lunch. While living at Wangford another snowstorm blocked all the roads in and out of Southwold. After dealing at first with everything by telephone I decided I could wait no longer. Farmer Kim Kent, living just outside Wangford, came to my rescue. Sitting high up in the cab of his huge tractor making our way, we even had to circumvent the snowdrift on the Wangford road. Entering Southwold up the High Street felt like the relief of Mafeking. The October storm of 1987 again blocked all the roads into Southwold, this time with fallen trees. It became impossible to get in even making my way over the fields.

Attending a GP refresher course, I was made to realise how lucky I was in one way as a country doctor. The psychiatrist giving a talk started by asking us what was our major problem. With one voice the town doctors' response was – traffic. Is this a reason that many doctors are now voting to stop visits?

## Stress

General practitioners in recent years are frequently complaining of the stress of their work. As a result some now, even in their forties, are reducing their days to four or even less a week. I wonder how they would have coped with being on call at nights and weekends. If it didn't happen too frequently one could bear it. When partner numbers went up from three to five it became more tolerable, especially for weekends. Night calls are different. When in the depth of sleep, getting one's brain to work asking question after question of the caller, trying to become alert enough to make a perhaps vital decision, can be difficult. If the request was a delivery or a straightforward pain in the chest, there was no problem. The child with a fever could be the most difficult to decide whether to visit or just give advice. After giving the latter, quite often it could be hard to get to sleep again, worrying whether you had made the right decision.

I think I suffered more from stress than I realised. It was in my late thirties that while walking up the steps from the beach to the house I felt a central chest pain. Could it be the start of angina or just an odd feeling of guilt as I had just been chatting to Dizzy Ogilvie lying on the beach? Waiting for it the next time I did any exertion, of course the chest pain recurred. It happened again if I was called to anyone suspected of a heart attack. While on a week's attachment at my old hospital, the chance of having an exercise ECG (that proved normal) didn't alleviate my worry, though I continued to play rugby. The problem reached a peak one evening at the age of 43. I had had a lot of extra worry at the cost of putting the very derelict Ford House (just bought) in order. Sitting watching a television programme about the North African campaign I had a recurrence of chest pain and felt my heart racing. Convinced I was having a heart attack and having something on my conscience I sent for Fr. Rudd. After he had gone, I felt at peace but then thought if I really believed I had had a heart attack I suppose I ought to send for a doctor. I phoned Doctor Borham as I had recently had an insurance medical with him. Admitted to the Norfolk and Norwich for 48 hours, I was reassured again. Time heals and the worry gradually subsided.

I wasn't a lone sufferer from anxiety. Later, when using hypnotherapy (described in detail later) I was asked by a GP to see one of her patients, a family doctor who was suffering from panic attacks when visiting patients. The referring GP had seen me demonstrating the use of hypnosis when she was my trainee. I saw my colleague once and taught him self-hypnosis with complete success. In my retirement he and his wife, also a GP, referred numerous patients with the same troubles to me for years. With so much talk of stressed doctors at present, could there be a better example of how this simple form of treatment can be so effective? Why is it so little used by medical professionals when they are crying out for help?

# Fun and Games

B
ut life wasn't all work and no play. Lucky enough to be living at Southwold and coastal Suffolk, we made the best of its beaches, rivers, broads, woodlands, heaths and countryside. We enjoyed our family life (increased by James in 1960 and William in 1963), a social life and of course holidays.

Southwold was an ideal place for a young family to grow up in. It felt very safe for them to have the freedom to roam around the town on their own, on bike or roller skate, having just its one road in and out. The crime rate in our early days was very low. In our first year, on leaving our house for a week without a front door key, we were told not to worry. Burglaries didn't happen in Southwold.

For their early schooling the children could go to the kindergarten run by Elizabeth Bonsey, daughter of the dear Canon, still in existence on South Green. Eversley Preparatory school on the Common, founded at Southwold at the turn of the century, was also still functioning for the boys. The children also went to the Southwold Primary school just behind us, where Tina had her first proposal in marriage. She did accept one later from an ex-Southwoldian, Lindsay Clubb, whose family made history when they sold their house facing the common. It went for what was then thought the outrageous price of £17,000. Nothing had been sold previously for over £10,000. It set the trend for the meteoric rise since.

Being so dedicated to starting up the practice in my early months, my only exercise was getting in and out of the car. I felt quite stiff after one day walking the few yards to the pier and back. It was not good enough.

In that first summer I did join the Southwold Cricket Club captained by John Cook. Thinking I must be good, having played for my school, he put me high on the batting list. After a series of miserable scores, I went further and further down the order.

## Swimming

Swimming was available just in front of us at North Parade. As soon as they learnt to swim, the children loved it. Many a summer morning they would come into our bedroom at 7.00am: "Can we go for a swim Daddy?" Perhaps I had been up half the night. I would drag myself out of my bed, but once in the sea, swimming as was our custom into the sunbeam over the water, was a delight. There were many other choices of beaches at Walberswick, Minsmere, Covehithe, or further afield on the Norfolk coast. It was one warm sunny day in February that they all asked if they could have a swim. I said not now but a sunny day in April. The sunny day came.

"You promised!"

"Alright, go in but I bet you won't stay in long." They didn't.

1959 was a particularly good summer; we had our first bathe at Minsmere on 1st May. The hot dry weather continued into the autumn. The sea remained very calm for periods. At one time on the front of North Parade the water became so clear we could see the remains of an old wreck on the seabed below. At low tide it was special fun to swim or wade out to a sand bank sometimes appearing over the surface of the water. It was unfortunately the cause of a tragedy when the children of the Beach Mission stayed out too long and got caught by the incoming tide. In panic one child gripped her carrier too tightly round the throat so that he collapsed fatally as he reached the shore.

## Riding

Riding was to play a large part in the family's enjoyment of life. Unfortunately Mary, although we had ridden together quite a lot in our early married life, lost her confidence, as so often happens with women after childbearing. We did hire horses from Jimmy Bugg's stable in Walberswick on our first summer. After our first canter over the common, seeing Mary laughing (it seemed for the first time since arrival at Southwold in January) made me realise what a strain it must all have been for her. When later I bought my horse Harlequin, she got on, he took off and landed her in a bush. She never rode again.

Harlequin was also to take off with a good friend of ours, David Mitchell, manager of Benacre Estate. As he walked beside me on the Southwold Common one summer afternoon I let him have a go. The next thing I knew, David was scattering the players on the cricket field, but luckily didn't spoil the crease going midway between the stumps.

Our first pony for the children was a gift from a patient. It was an elderly grey called Snowy. Keeping it in a field at Blythburgh, we decided we would bring her to Southwold and use her for children's rides at our church fete. With Frances on her back we reached the Bailey Bridge via the old railway track. Snowy then completely refused to go over. With us was Bruce Kent, a mutual old friend from London. (He had once taken Mary to an Oxford ball before joining the priesthood and later to be Chairman of CND.) Between us we reversed Snowy and inch by inch, with our shoulders to hers, pushed her as in a scrum over to the other side. We tethered her in our back garden and then three days later, to the delight of children, gave rides at the fete on the common.

Snowy didn't last long. She developed a cancer and had to be put down. An advertisement in the EDP brought Glitter, a Connemara pony to us. In her time she had taught a series of families to ride. We rented a field from the Southwold Borough Council at the far end of the common. With a shed to store hay and a shelter for the horses it was ideally situated to enable the years of excitement that followed. The girls Frances and Tina, aged around 10 years, had two or so lessons at the Pakefield riding school, and then went straight off on their pony to canter and have fun. Joined by Jane Ogilvie and other girls (riding is much more favoured by the fairer sex), they were soon exploring across the common onto the beach or over the Bailey Bridge to the world beyond. There they had at their disposal the Walberswick common and the old railway line to Blythburgh. In between the school holidays, I also joined in with a loan of Copper from Jimmy

Bugg's stable. Our area then expanded to the Walberswick marshes, the Dunwich forest and heath. A really good canter, splashing through the edge of the sea, was along the beach past Eastern Bavants to Covehithe, with Mary meeting us there by car to have a swim and picnic. Riding on the beach in front of Southwold was allowed then with the groynes making splendid jumps.

There were very few walkers in the sixties and seventies on the footpaths and dyke tops around Walberswick and Dunwich. I instructed the girls to be very polite if they met anyone on a footpath to say, "Good morning." They then wouldn't object. There was a notice at the Bailey Bridge that read, "No horses across the bridge," to which the children said, "Well it doesn't say anything about ponies does it?" I took my horse across as I felt it was a good test to show it was then quite safe for those on foot. On one occasion, to make a short cut, I drove over in my Morris Minor. I must have been spotted as shortly afterwards a bollard was put up. A gate was put up across the dyke top path near the burnt-out mill on the Walberswick marshes, presumably to discourage us. It made another splendid jump.

Harlequin, a three-year-old bay belonging to Melody Cross at the Harbour Inn, came on the market for £200 including tack. Very appropriately I had just been left this sum by a patient I hardly knew. Harlequin was to prove my great joy for the next 16 years. I taught him to jump; he taught me how to jump. Dunwich forest on many occasions became our base where we camped to have fun on our horses and explore beyond. One of these times was to ride on past Minsmere beach to Sizewell and down to Thorpeness. The Ogilvie connection was useful in finding a field for our rides, while we dipped into the indoor swimming pool existing then.

Dunwich forest became the battleground in a game that I organized. It was to be a war between the Romans and the British tribesmen. To quote the order of battle: "The Romans in their settlement at Southwold, having been attacked for many years by the marauding British tribesmen dwelling in the forest of Dunwich, are determined once and for all to get rid of this menace by destroying them in their base. Who will win the battle? The brave well-disciplined Romans or the wily and expert horsemen in the forest?"

The two Onyett girls, Wendy and Trish from Brook Farm Wenhaston and Jane Blanchflower, daughter of the Southwold Lloyds Bank manager, were part of the Roman team. Frances, Tina, Jane Ogilvie and me were part of the Brits. Both sides were armed with lances, long poles but with strict instructions not to sharpen them. The main object was for the Romans to get into the base made up in the main long ride and both sides to make as many 'kills' as possible. I realised what it was like to be chased by a lancer when I heard the thundering hooves of an Onyett girl's horse getting closer and closer as I was trying to urge my Harlequin on, waiting for that prod in the back. I can't remember who won but it was fun despite the rain pouring down.

James came of age and started to join in the riding. It was fairly early on when encouraged by his over enthusiastic father he took a jump and fell.

"I've hurt my arm Daddy!"

"Get back on that pony."

The pain persisted on returning from the field. James insists that I tested him by asking him to open the car door. He couldn't – so to Southwold hospital and an X-ray that revealed a greenstick fracture of the humerus. Have I been forgiven?

Tina was to sustain a much more serious fracture. Sitting on friend Jane's pony, it reared over backwards. Tina still in the saddle, it landed on top of her. With the expert help of partner Graham Bracewell, she was X-rayed at Southwold to show a fractured pelvis. As Graham was carrying her up the stairs at North Parade, I was in the loo just realising the two-day flu I had been suffering from was in fact Infective Hepatitis. Poor Mary had two invalids on her hands. These two incidents just go to show how blessed we were in those days with facilities so close to home at Southwold. No need for a 20-mile journey and wait in A&E.

Tina was not long back in the saddle. Later she joined the hunt on Glitter and later still on Harlequin. Frances, rather diffidently, was the first to hunt. She preferred to dismount at every ditch to lead her pony across rather than stay on. William in his turn was very quick to get into riding and soon became the darling at the pony club. James would have joined the club but developed appendicitis on the eve. I was to send three of my children to have an appendicectomy by my former anatomy teacher at the Middlesex Hospital, Bernard Hand. Not always the case with medical parents, but I chose to look after my young as I trusted myself more in the practice than anyone else, other than Graham for orthopaedics.

On one occasion I did scare myself treating my own. James having a severe attack of hay fever one evening I gave him some Piriton without looking up the dosage for his age. Too late I checked it, to discover to my horror that I had overdosed him to a large degree. Feeling I had to watch over him I had an anxious night sleeping on the floor beside his bed. He slept soundly and woke next morning bright and breezy.

With the encouragement of Ian Finch of Manor Farm, Henham, I was soon to join in my first hunt with the Waveney Harriers. Harlequin rapidly learnt to be one of the best jumpers of ditches. On several occasions the master Lord Somerleyton would say, "Give us a lead, Hopkins." Before long I earned the title of the galloping doctor. But it had been a poor start at our first hunter trials. Refusing twice on each obstacle, we only just got round to the last jump. This was a water trough. It was a hot spring day. Harlequin utterly refused to jump it. All he was interested in was to have a drink. He was to be eliminated later at another hunter trial for being too keen. It was a five-bar gate. We were supposed to come up to it, open it by hand, go through and then close it. I couldn't stop him jumping it. I thought to turn round, jump back over again, open the gate by hand and close, I would be doing the right thing but was immediately ordered off the course.

Being a medical man on the hunt had its uses. At a hunter trial in the middle of Henham Park our master Colonel Tomkin fell and was concussed. But arranging an ambulance I was humbled by the fact I had to ask the attending vet if I could use his mobile phone. Vets had them long before doctors. I was also in attendance at a hunt when Brigadier Bill Carr keeled over dead from his horse beside me, still holding onto his riding crop.

I did on a few occasions revert to ancient medical practice by going on horseback to patients. Apart from the enjoyment I felt, I could then claim tax relief for the hay. Blythburgh was the most accessible when living at Southwold. Using the old railway track, I rode there on a last visit on my half day. Some relatives were especially pleased when I rode to Walberswick to sign the second half of a cremation certificate. They said the dead person had been mad about horses.

## Shooting

To paraphrase George Orwell, an old Southwoldian himself, all patients are equal, but some are more equal than others. It was in the autumn of my second year that Clidy Johnson came into the Blythburgh branch surgery. Somehow, we got onto the subject of shooting and at the end of it he invited me to come shooting on his land whenever I wanted. He had over a thousand acres scattered in different parts all over the countryside, with his home farm at Bramfield. We started at Laxfield, the family coming too, in the days when there were still large coveys of wild partridge. On one occasion a huge one came up out of the sugar beet. You would have thought it impossible to miss with two of us using both barrels, but not one came down. Photos of Frances and Tina on those early days show them holding up a pheasant each almost as big as themselves.

We had a series of golden retrievers whom I did my best to train as gun dogs. Our first one, Dusty, came to us rushing through the gate with the rest of the litter into our back garden from the Craighurst hotel next door. We made a big fuss of them. Later that day the owners, who were patients of mine, offered us the gift of one, and so the most affectionate of dogs came to be with us. For the next fourteen years Dusty grew to be my constant companion on my rounds. At Blythburgh hospital he was a big favourite with the patients, taking to lying under the bed whenever I had to examine anyone.

Training him with a dummy on the common I thought at first it had to be done with rewards and kindness, but to no avail. The biscuit did not work. Eventually, getting cross, I gave him a cuff over the head with an instant good result. But on my first excursion with Dusty, firing and seeing a pheasant drop down ahead, as I turned round to urge him forward, there was my gun dog fleeing backwards for all his worth. He soon got the idea, with any shot anywhere, he wanted to be after it. Just seeing me getting my gun out at home would get him really worked up. My shooting, apart from the family and on occasions with a friend John Hashim, was alone and for the pot. On one occasion setting out to get our Sunday lunch, I was returning empty handed when just short of Southwold a pheasant crashed into the windscreen and saved the day.

I did get a few invitations for more formal shoots. On a shoot that the already mentioned John Levell-Scrivener invited me to, I had a stand on a drive with my back to the old Abbey ruins. My birds kept dropping behind me into where in times past the monks prayed. John was passionate about shooting and hated the hunt although his wife Juliet took part. When the Waveney Harriers met on an adjoining estate, he made one stipulation that they were not to ride through his covers. As happened, they went straight into his best wood. John, standing at the end when they came out, vented all his anger at the master Colonel Tomkins. His language was like a trooper at the best of times. Trying to get through to John myself, I don't think he saw me for the blueness of the air around him. Another invitation came after I was asked to do an insurance medical for John Hill MP. I heard his solicitor was a little amazed but delighted when I pronounced him fit There followed an invitation to a Boxing day shoot and many others.

On becoming teenagers, the children joined in. It was Tina who made our day once with the single-barrelled four ten. Lord Gladwyn and a friend joined us on the Home Farm. He had recently bought Bramfield Hall and tended to just turn up on occasions. With the four of us surrounding a spinney, a pheasant came out in front of me then circled around in front of the other guns, all having at least one shot, until on the far side a little pop from Tina and down the bird came. We were invited to tea at the Hall on the strength of it. It was James later who rather went off shooting aged about 18. He reluctantly came, then became more and more frustrated after missing with one shot after another. That made him more determined, until he couldn't wait to get a bird. He never looked back, being the good shot he is now.

# Rugby

Having a beer at the bar in The Harbour Inn after a sail with my old school mate Michael Hardy, himself a former stand off for England, we overheard two fellows talking about rugby. They were planning to start a rugby club at Southwold in the coming season. I was to find later they were Brian Barnes and Gavin Sneddon. I pricked up my ears and as we were leaving, I intruded and offered my services to the club as a full back. Now thirty-seven, I thought I'd hung up my boots for good at thirty on arrival at Southwold from my last season, when playing as a three quarter in London Club Rugby. So started a further seven years of the game. I think I scored as many tries at full back as in the three quarters.

Our opening game on our pitch on Southwold Common with Peter Kemsley our skipper was against Ipswich. Only just arrived from Dublin, Bernard Seagrave Daly, later to become Managing Director of Adnams, was put in the Ipswich side to make up their numbers. Coming into the line and selling Bernard a dummy, he took it. Racing through, then running out of steam, the police constable in our side coming alongside took a pass to score the try that equalised the match. I was able to see all this that evening on the Anglia television. It was a good start to seven years of enjoyable rugby. I was in the team for the Norwich sevens that first season. On one round we beat the West Norfolk club captained by Mary's cousin Tim Ruane, so I was able to crow about it for ever after. Playing on the exposed position of the common we did often experience some strong winds. The pitch being east-west facing then, one time, kicking off from the centre against an easterly gale, the ball sailed up into the air over the 10-yard line in front, soared further up and then back over our heads to end up behind our dead ball line.

My obliging partner Graham, standing in for me when on duty, enabled me to play an extra number of home games, his fee a bottle of sherry if he was called out. One famous occasion when I was knocked out lying on the ground, the opposition asked, "Isn't there a doctor in the team?"

My mates answered, "Yes. Down there on the ground".

The good Bernard helped me off the pitch, me murmuring, "Am I married?" I never could understand what I meant by that.

However not all my patients liked the thought of their doctor playing this rough game. I know one old lady, living in a grand house in Lorne Road, in particular didn't. Maybe this added to our contretemps later. Asking me to pay a call, she stipulated not in the morning as she was going to the hairdresser in Halesworth. When I crossly said then why couldn't she come to see me she took herself off my list.

My last game of rugby in April 1971 came. Stephen Marshlain the skipper, when a try had been scored in the corner at the last moment, asked me to take the kick – something I didn't normally do. To my delight the ball soared into the air but then went inches outside the posts and the final whistle blew. It could have been such a fitting end.

We saw a lot of Bernard in the early days. As a bachelor living round the corner in Church Street, we semi-adopted him. On several nights when he had finished his studies for an accounting exam he would come round late at night for bacon and egg cooked by Mary. On many an occasion he came to babysit for us. One time leaving our surgery house late in the evening he was seen by a policeman doing his tour of the town. Southwold had residual policemen in those days. The PC accosted Bernard with: "Tut tut! Fancy bothering the doctor at this hour." Bernard was to lead me astray on St Patrick's night. Taking me to the King's Head that was holding a special Irish do, I drank too much Guinness. I had to pay for it the next morning at my surgery with a ghastly hangover. "I think you look more ill than I do," said several patients. I eventually had to make an excuse to go to the bathroom.

Later at the Rugger Club dinner at The Crown, I tried to get my own back on Bernard by getting his face slapped. Susan Doy was a waitress. As she was serving Bernard, I gave her bottom a pinch. Unfortunately, another waitress spotted me and gave the game away. Susan, who later became Mayor of Southwold, never took offence. For years after my retirement she continued sending me a Christmas card saying I was her best doctor. Bernard ended his bachelor days by marrying Oonagh. Mary and I went to the wedding in London. Exactly nine months later Oonagh gave birth to their first child. She was certainly a fast worker. I never did manage to get to Oonagh's next two home deliveries in time.

# Sailing

As one sport came to an end another could take over. One of them was sailing. It was something I had done a lot of in my student days, either in dinghies or crewing offshore. I had taken part in most RORC races except for the Fastnet. Early in our time at Southwold, sitting on a Brittany shore on holiday there (subsidised by a friend of Mary's family), I remember looking wistfully out to sea, longing to be out there again. Little did I realise we had just started an offspring who in his early twenties was going to take me to the Mediterranean in his yacht. A cheeky patient of mine when he heard the date of the expected delivery said he would be wearing a Breton beret.

Our friend John Hashim had let us make use of his Wayfarer he kept at Slaughden Quay on the Alde. Taking it out at the time of our camping holidays with the horses in Dunwich forest, it had doubled our sport. Then, with land to keep a dinghy on the premises on coming to Wangford, I bought an Enterprise in 1972. These were renowned for being very capsizeable, something I had never experienced. I was soon to find it out at our first outing with the four children on board at Oulton Broad. With buildings and trees surrounding it on all sides the wind comes from every direction. Whoops, and the four were under the sail. The water was shallow so you could stand up but the family has teased me about it ever since.

I was later to change to a more sturdy Wayfarer. Keeping it at the Aldeburgh Yacht Club then meant we had 10 miles of the Alde river to explore. Using the ebb tide we sailed down to Orford for lunch and a drink at the Jolly Sailor, or with the rising tide to Iken Broad and beyond to Snape and the Plough and Sail. Little Japan on the Broad was a favourite spot for a picnic and a swim, as on the sandy beach further up the river. There Mary could meet us by car. The last part to Snape usually meant much tacking one way or another. On several occasions we made an evening sail with two other families, the Hashims and Wheelers, barbequing on the shore of the Broad and returning with all the excitement in the gathering dark.

It was taking three of our family and Paul Hashim back from upriver, late in the afternoon in early September, that as we entered the far end of the Broad, a heavy mist came down with visibility reduced to just a few yards. It could have spelled disaster. The passage winds across the Broad and with the tide fast running out, at any moment we could have got stuck with the prospect of floundering in the mud to find the shore. Luckily I remembered that occasion in my student days, entering the Crouch Estuary in the dark on returning from the Continent. With no lights and no sat-nav then, the clever navigator took us in by taking soundings, feeling the bottom and zig-zagging in. When the water went down to two metres or so we went about at a right angle and so on. I did the same in the Wayfarer as we rowed across the Broad feeling the bottom with an oar. It was a great relief when eventually we came across the racing buoy marking the entrance to the river at the far end and knew we had made it.

On one quite windy day, James, William and myself made our way down river past Orford to Butley Creek, tacking all the way. After a respite to refresh ourselves at a landing stage there we returned back for home to discover the wind had reverted in completely the opposite direction. Having to take the tiller the whole time as my crew were too young to take it in the conditions, by the time we got back to Orford I felt quite exhausted. Suggesting to the boys that perhaps we could stop there and take a taxi back to Aldeburgh, they would have none of it. Despite being perpetually sprayed in the front of the boat as they dealt with the jib sheets, they were enjoying themselves. After another hour of hard tacking it was a great relief to be back at the club.

A good sense of smell can be a great asset. This was particularly so for James that his father had this sensitivity as it resulted in him starting on the path to being the great entrepreneur that he is. I was seeing a patient of mine who I thought was in the agricultural business, when I realised he smelt of fish. Enquiring if he had been on the beach fishing, he said no, he had changed his job to now selling fish. He bought it at Lowestoft fish market then took it in a van to do a round of villages near Cambridge. He was doing quite well and mentioned someone else at Southwold doing the same had now earned enough to buy a yacht. Just mentioning this to James by way of conversation as we were sailing on the Alde a day or so later, he asked me seriously if could I introduce him to the patient. At this time aged 19, having no particular job, he was rolling out the barrels for Adnams brewery. The net result was that he developed his own fish round in Essex and within two years he had acquired his yacht and a TR7 sports car to boot.

Our first trip together was from Orford, where he based his yacht the Sunitu, to Ostend. Our navigator was a friend/patient, Frank Hawkins, a former merchant seaman. I always said he did his navigation on a match box. I was looking after his wife Cynthia who had terminal cancer at the time. I was especially pleased that I had made her a self-hypnosis tape with a Chopin musical accompaniment. She was dying with severe jaundice but didn't realise it. But when told the facts she went completely euphoric. I have never seen anyone die so happily.

Walking along a street in Cambridge, three to four months before Cynthias's death, I saw through an open door a man giving a lecture. I entered to find he was enthusing about a dietary method of dealing with cancer. Thinking of Cynthia, I tackled him at the end to discover he lived at Diss. When I discussed this with Frank and Cynthia, they went to see him. He was not charging any fee, just a donation. However, like many of these therapies, the diet was difficult to follow. Cynthia tried it for a while and then gave it up.

On this subject of dietary therapy for cancer, I was impressed by a lecture at the Royal College of Medicine in London given by a woman who herself had suffered from breast cancer with secondary spread not responding to treatment. She did some research to realise the low rate of breast cancer in China could be explained by their very low intake of dairy products. Completely avoiding milk and its products, her cancer and metastases went into remission and had remained so for the past ten years since. She preached the idea to other sufferers to get the same good result. She also mentioned cancer of the prostate could be helped in the same way. I did try the soya milk substitute myself to see what it was like. I think I would have to be *in extremis* to use it.

James, after two to three years in the fish business, decided he had had enough. Before changing occupation with sufficient in the kitty, he took time off to take Sunitu via the rivers and canals of France to the

Mediterranean. I joined him on the Seine at Rouen to have a trip through delightful unspoilt country, past Monet's garden to Paris, staying there in a basin just under Notre Dame. James by this time was getting very good at manoeuvring Sunitu through the locks despite the hazard of the dismasted mast protruding many feet over the stern. I had phoned ahead to our French friends the Fruchauds (to be mentioned later) to join us for a drink on board. In turn we were invited to their *apartement* in the Latin Quarter to make, as Tatiana put it, our own supper – a fondue. We continued on up the even more tree-lined Marne, many trees festooned with bunches of mistletoe, to the champagne country at Chalons. There I had to make my way back to England and work. James made his way on from the river Marne through the connecting tunnel to the Rhone and onto the Mediterranean near Marseille. After he had sailed along the Cote d'Azure and down the Italian coast, William and I caught up with him again by train from England in July at the Messina Straits.

En route, meeting us at the station at Rome was Francesco to give us a night stop over. (I had got to know him when he was living as an au pair with Iris Birtwhistle and her three adopted boys at Walberswick. Iris had taken him on after seeing his advert in The Times. Iris was a quite eccentric single woman who ran a small art gallery and had old Amplefordian brothers. She was one of the few who made the reverse move of joining my practice on account of my faith on my arrival at Southwold. She surprised me on one occasion when inviting Mary and me to an art exhibition in her house. We entered the drawing room to find, without any previous warning, Benjamin Britten and Peter Pears standing by the fire in the otherwise empty room. They offered no conversation to us and I was non-plussed how to open one. Does one say, "Have you heard any good music lately?" Iris also took under her wing Jenny Lash, the authoress, who married local farmer Mark Fiennes and gave birth to two well-known actors, Ralph and Joseph.)

Francesco let us loll around through the day by the pool at the back of his block of flats, a much-needed rest after our overnight travel. In the evening after supper, with his mother and two attractive young girl cousins, Francesco took us on a tour of the city ending with a romantic view of the Forum in the moonlight. He generously gave us the use of his flat to sleep in while he moved out. He was a most warm-hearted and jovial man typical of his country.

From the Messina Straits we made our way in a dead calm to the Greek island of Kefalonia. One memorable sight was huge swordfish swimming alongside. Going through the port authorities at Kefalonia, we were reminded of troubles in South Italy when an Italian yacht owner handed in his revolver for the time he was there. He said he had to carry a weapon when sailing in Italian waters as he had once been kidnapped and had to pay a ransom to the mafia to be released. We made further anchorage in a small bay on the other side of the island and then to the legendary island of Ithaca, of Odysseus fame. All three ports of call had excellent restaurants ashore to taste the Greek food and drink. Our final sail onto the island of Paxos and then Corfu were the only passages with a fair wind.

An overnight ferry took me back to the Italian mainland at Bari to start me on my way home. For the whole day's journey by train up the East coast I was in the delightful company of three Italian girl veterinary students. They did their best to improve my Italian. Hearing I came from Suffolk they tried to tell me about what sounded to me like "a Suffolk ship" until the penny dropped it was "Suffolk sheep"! One very friendly signorina, even though being met on the platform at Bologna by her fiancé, still insisted on giving me a fond farewell embrace in front of him. James made the voyage back through the Messina Straits, encountering heavy storms off the island of Stromboli. Making the port of Bonafacio on the South end of Corsica, he left Sunitu to winter there. He returned to pick it up the next year in the summer to make his way back through the canals of France to emerge near Calais and finally, like a returning Frances Drake, sailed back into Southwold harbour.

## Tennis

On buying Ford House I saw my chance of having my own tennis court. There was enough room in the old kitchen garden to bulldoze a lawn court. With the help of my father, who had been a top club player in his time, we got the measurements right and sowed the seed, when my generous mother-in-law offered to pay for a much more useful hard court. There was room in the adjoining field to make it. It has been my boon and joy ever since then to be still playing three sets a week now in my 93rd year (at the time of writing). To begin with it was mixed doubles with Mary until sadly her arthritis set in. The children, and in turn grandchildren, have made good use of it. Mary Pretty (a player for Suffolk and later a senior for Great Britain), living in the village when we arrived, gave William coaching lessons, he being the only one then not at boarding school. Hence, he is the one with style that his un-coached father certainly lacks.

To the great joy of families around, I organised for several years a family tennis tournament to take place on one afternoon in the first week of the summer holidays. Four courts of four family homes took part. Each held their own knock out tournament, with pairs made up by adult and child. In the preliminary rounds at each house, everyone played everyone for five games and the winning pair was decided by the one achieving the most games. To keep all the players active, I organised a simultaneous tournament in croquet, badminton and boules – a truly active afternoon. The winning pair then had a semi-final between two courts and the final in one of the four courts, with all joining in to watch and enjoy a grand tea. The first year William and I played together and reached the final to play against the two Johns, Hashim and Wheeler. We won. On another year, having changed the rules, I played with Hazel Parker, an old family friend. We didn't reach anywhere. The final was at the Cranfield's, who had a swimming pool. In a fit of exuberance, I picked up my attractive partner and jumped with her, both of us fully clothed, into the water.

The tournament continued under the auspices of the local Red Cross, thanks to John Veitch organising and Keith and Jill Skinner holding the final in their garden with a bumper tea. I also took part in a tournament organised by the Ipswich Red Cross branch with Mary Pretty as my partner. When we won, taking away each a bottle of champagne, the locals were furious on discovering I had brought a Suffolk and GB champion. It was made clear she was not to come again.

# Skiing

Taking up a sport in later life has one great advantage. To improve over one's later years, when if you had started at an early age your skill would be deteriorating, is great for the morale. I could only start taking skiing holidays at the age of 55 as only then could I afford it, our last offspring having left boarding school. Although William was now starting his medical studies, in the 1980s students not only had no tuition fees, but were given a maintenance allowance, even with relatively well-off parents.

So, in the spring of 1983 I arranged our first skiing holiday in the French Alps for Mary, Frances, William and myself. Having booked this around Christmas for April, Frances in the interval gave the news she was pregnant for the first time and worried if she should go. I reassured her that when her mother and I had a skiing weekend while doing my National Service in Germany, she herself was there in the early stages of existence and both came to no harm. I continued skiing every year until I was eighty, continuing to improve my skills on the slopes into my seventies. I would probably be foolish enough to be at it now if it hadn't been for the need to care for Mary.

# Golf

With a golf course on the Common at Southwold, reputedly the second to originate in the county after Aldeburgh, the reader will wonder if I didn't mention the sport. It is supposed to be the most favoured pastime of the medical profession. If a doctor is accused of neglecting his practice, it is often blamed on the fact that he is spending too much time on the golf course. The truth for me is that I am hopeless at the game and it has not been for the want of trying. After joining the Highgate Golf Club as a weekly member for our two-week stay at Mary's parents early on arrival at Southwold, I became keen enough to join the Southwold Club. But not finding time to play, I gave it up. On retirement, thinking I could get into the game with more time on my hands, I joined the newly founded club at Halesworth. But even several coaching lessons made little effect.

Encouraged at first, I managed to get a good friend, John Holmes, to join me, saying, "We are playing tennis together now in our sixties, but surely this won't last into our seventies and eighties, when really old codgers still play golf." Little did I realise that we would both be playing tennis in our nineties and for me golf has been long given up. After laughing at John's first efforts doing even worse than me, he went to the pro Harry at his own club, Aldeburgh. He came back hitting the ball down the fairway. I thought this could also be my answer, but sadly could not get the same Harry effect.

Keeping the family honour, however, it is Mary who is the golfer. When at the Southwold Golf Club on social occasions, I proudly stand in front of Mary's name on two of the boards to get the reflected glory. William's housemaster at Ampleforth, Father Edward Corbould, a very sporting monk, came to stay at Ford House while doing a wedding at Beccles. On the Saturday morning I took him on at tennis and lost. On the Monday, Mary took Father Edward round the Southwold golf course to get a par on every hole and beat him. He has never got over it. Father Edward in fact was born not far away at the village of Lound, the other side of Lowestoft. His father was rector there. When his father went over to Rome he had to leave. Father Edward was sent to school at Ampleforth and stayed on as a monk. His father's name was erased from the list of rectors on the board inside the church. In better days it has now been reinstated, but the smudge marks remain.

## Social Life

Not long after we arrived, Bruce and Dizzy Ogilvie very kindly started us off by organising a special party in April for us to meet all their social friends. (Bruce was a doctor in the opposite Southwold practice.) There we met the Priors, Yates and Montagus, all farmers, amongst others. We later met more farmers – the Holmes and Mitchells. Being of our age with children to match meant in the course of time several family parties. These occurred especially at Christmas, all living in big houses, taking turns every year.

In my turn I organised a car treasure hunt in the summer. Five families took part meeting at the start at the White Hart Blythburgh, the children dressed as pirates. I had boxes with different clues, all described in doggerel, dotted about the countryside. The one I especially liked went – *As Charon takes you o'er the Styx, find this man in Walberswick.* It was the ferryman of course. But Clifford Russell an architect friend (paralysed crossing the Rhine in his tank in WW2), driving one car with some of our family on board, misread 'Styx' as 'sticks'. Thinking of my love of riding, he went first to Jimmy Bugg's stables. Another clue took you to Blythburgh geriatric hospital, where I had one of its old able-bodied inmates sit on the low wall outside with a buttonhole to distinguish him. Another dozen of the old boys came to sit with him with similar buttonholes causing confusion for the contestants. Under a straw stack in the middle of Blythburgh village I arranged a body – trousers with boots on and upper garments all stuffed with straw emerging from the straw. Sticking out of the chest with ketchup dripping down from it was a knife. A lad working for Bob Aldred, whose stack it was, came across the "body". In horror he reported it to Bob who reassured him: "It's only the doctor having his bit of fun." Each car was directed in a different order of clues so as not to follow one another but they were all directed to a final clue – Veronica Gerrell dressed as a fisherman sitting on a bench in front of the Sailor's Reading Room in Southwold. This sent them to the treasure installed at the Harbour Inn. The Priors were the first to arrive and open the tin chest filled with sweets, money and a bottle for the parents. Everyone was given a sealed envelope with the final destination inside in case they didn't make it, but all made it for tea and drinks in time. Dan Yates was caught speeding through Blythburgh. The officer on asking Dan what he was doing was given the facetious reply, "I'm a pirate."

The Yates organised another game in the summer on their farm. This was a battle. It is difficult to remember what happened. Perhaps it had something to do with the very strong rounds of G&T that the parents were supplied with before battle commenced.

Weddings are a great chance for a good party. At Ford House we have held six so far. With a garden leading to within ten yards of the porch of the parish church, St Peter and Paul, and the choice of the two lawns large enough for marquees, we are ideally situated. Frances and Tina were the first to be wedded. Our Wangford vicar Miles Copley did the actual marriage ceremony for Tina and our good friend Tim Hollis of the Sotterley parish for Frances, as Miles was away at the time. But saying the Nuptial Mass on both occasions was our old friend from our London days, Monsignor Bruce Kent. We reckoned it was the first Mass to be said in the Wangford church since the Reformation. Times have certainly changed since I was a young boy.

The wedding lunch on both occasions took place in a marquee on the larger lawn followed by a disco in the evening, one of the all too few times that the bride's father can let himself go. Both days were blessed with wonderful weather.

James's first marriage had to take place at a registry office as his bride had been briefly married before. The Rev Harry Edwards, vicar of Reydon Church, performed a blessing service at Blythburgh Church. (Harry had had his connection to Ampleforth , having been attached to the monastery there for a year before being ordained in the Anglican Church.) James also used a marquee at Ford House for his wedding supper.

William and Jane chose to do things differently by having a marriage in Wangford Church in the evening in winter. They emerged from the church in the dark to lead the guests through the garden gate from the porch, walking between flares on the lawn down to the house and through to a marquee on the terrace lawn.

A granddaughter, Mary Jane, chose to follow her parents, Lindsay and Tina, with a Wangford church wedding and reception in the garden. The house with its large reception rooms has made the ideal venue for many a party starting with our house warming, children's parties and to celebrate the later decades as they pass. Ford House, with the family enlarged with thirteen grandchildren and three greats, can still lend itself to family occasions. I bless the day I knocked on its door.

# The French Circle

With my great love of languages and French in particular, I started a French Circle at Ford House in 1980. It has flourished since. Meetings take place every month or so at different people's homes or a pub very informally. The only rule – English is *tout a fait interdit* for the evening. I was made *le président* for the first thirteen years and as a result at the time had made more speeches in my life in French than in English. In its early days in particular it was the cause of much fun. We enjoyed singing many of the French songs of the earlier part of the century such as Madame la Marquise, Le Fiacre and La Mer. For the *dîner de Noël* I made up songs about the Anglo-French scene – on one occasion, myself as François Mitterand and Pat Romer Grundy as Madame Thatcher meeting up in the tunnel of love (representing the newly opened Channel Tunnel), all to the tune of "Don't cry for me, Argentina." Lady Caroline Blois, a professional accompanist, was on the piano. For the past ten years we have held more serious literary evenings starting with Proust, continuing with all the 19th century authors that I like so much – Maupassant, Flaubert, Zola – and now reading Molière plays. My love of reading French had begun in my student days. On asking my father what book he could recommend to start on that would keep my interest, he said Clochemerle.

For those who don't know it, it concerns a conflict in a small French country town about the instillation next to the church of a *pissoir*. I did read it through. I thanked the circle at my 90th birthday party for the means of keeping my brains going.

If a French person came to my surgery, I used the opportunity to take them on in their own language. On one occasion I was given a lesson by a six-year-old girl with her mother. When I asked her her name in the English fashion – "Qu'est-ce que tu t'appelles?" "What do you call yourself?") – she immediately corrected me to "Comment tu t'appelles?" – ("How do you call yourself?") I have never forgotten my lesson.

# Holidays

Doctors today on an annual income of around £100,000 will be amazed that I started on £2000 with 10 years to parity. Undoubtedly houses were much cheaper to buy then but it still meant we couldn't afford even package holidays. Five years later as a result of Peter Westall leaving for the Anglican ministry, I became a senior partner. But deciding to educate our children privately, especially with boarding school fees, we still hadn't the means until later when they were off our hands.

Our early holidays were to stay at Mary's parent's comfortable home in Highgate. With the garden leading onto the second tee of the Highgate Golf Club I spent some of the time trying to learn the game. It was a good opportunity to catch up with our old London friends, meeting up to eat out in Soho. When Jim Prior became an MP in 1960 he joined us. On one occasion he had to leave us in the middle of supper to go back to the House when a division was called.

Jim took us with his wife Jane around the House of Commons and on to the Cabaret club. I was struck by how small the chamber looked and how near the opposing benches confronted each other. We in our turn, took them to a club in Soho that I had joined as a student, The Mandrake. Situated underground in a street named Meard Street and seeming to spread amongst the sewers of London, Jim was quite sure there would be a raid from the drug squad, and he would be in the news. I also took Jim on at golf to realise how business is conducted. At lunch at the club he offered to take me on as a director at a new company he was starting in Halesworth. Luckily for me it came to nothing. It was right out of my sphere.

For many of our other holidays we went camping or caravanning. As mentioned already we had great fun camping with the horse and pony in Dunwich forest. We also made it to the Yorkshire coast with a stopover on the way at the Gilling Lakes, once owned by my uncle Hugh Fairfax Cholmeley. A special reason to stay was for James to see across the valley the buildings of Ampleforth where he was to start boarding school in two years' time. I remember him looking at the buildings and saying rather proudly, that was where he was going to be. (Little did he realise how tough life was going to be in his first year at Junior House. But perhaps this helped to form the determined, independent person he became.) Our destination was Runswick Bay to join up with the Bunting family. John was now the art master at Ampleforth. On the journey the caravan and car being overloaded meant the children had to get out whenever we came to hills.

Keen to make the Continent one year, we loaded the car roof rack with camping gear. However, in the end we only had to set the tent up once. Invited to stay with the Purves family at Bern where Grant was the British consul, through friends of theirs we were lent the use of a caravan when we moved on to a site in the Alps. I have to say Libby, then a typical teenager was a bit reticent; she didn't want to speak to us grown-ups but has certainly made up for it on her radio programmes.

We were especially fortunate that several people lent us their houses. Jill Freud, whose children I had cared for when on holiday at Walberswick, very generously let us stay for two glorious weeks at her house on the island of Islay. She apologised when afterwards she had to sell it, as her husband Clement on becoming the Liberal MP in Norfolk felt it unseemly to have four houses now they had to set up another in his constituency.

1968 was the best summer Ireland had experienced for a century when Mary's mother hired a ranch sized bungalow on the shores of Loch Corrib for the family. The weather was so different from the continuous rain when cycling round it in 1946. Our attempts at fishing on the Loch and rivers came to very little, but rowing out to the many islands to picnic and swim was most enjoyable. We were to come across evidence of Mary's father's family origins in western Ireland on one of our excursions seeing a hotel named Mc Dowell.

Dr Pat Besley of the Halesworth Practice, who shared my round at the Blythburgh Hospital, also let us have the use of his cottage in Scotland near Ben Nevis at a very modest rent. The whole family, now teenagers, came. The great event was to climb Britain's highest mountain. Reading about it in a very old guidebook, which put out many alarming warnings, we treated it with great caution. On the day we took the path to the top we discovered every man and woman, some with lap dogs on a lead, were accompanying us quite casually as if on a Sunday stroll.

We were asked through some mutual friends to have the son of a French couple living in Cannes to stay, with the idea of William paying an exchange visit later with them. So Pierre Baelen came to us. He, poor fellow, like Anne and me those years ago having to go back to school while on holiday in England from our French Cairo school, joined William at the Eversley Prep school in Southwold for the last two weeks of term. He used every opportunity though to improve his serve on our tennis court, hoping no doubt to represent France one day. But as William didn't want to return the visit, a succession of invitations came from Pierre's mother Eliane for us to stay at their *apartement* in Cannes whilst they were away at their villa in St Tropez during the summer holiday. This we did on at least two occasions, coupling it with a stay on the way at partner Graham's holiday residence at a charming spot near Apt in Provence. He had converted an outbuilding in a farmyard. With other buildings around the yard used for holidaying by other French people, and the French farmer's family living in the farmhouse, it made a most convivial set up and great for my French. Invited by the farmer to join in the celebrations for a baptême and staying long into the night after Mary had left, I found on return to our building I was locked out. I had to sleep on the top of the outside stone steps (le perron), the cause of much amusement all round. Backing my car into the side of a nurse from Lyons's Deux Chevaux produced more invitations to drinks at her prettily converted cowshed.

The Baelens couldn't have been more charming. On our first visit we had lunch at their villa at St Tropez on the way there. At Cannes it was the musical festival. Jean Baelen being its president (he had retired from being the French Ambassador in the Lebanon), he arranged for us to have tickets to the music and ballet events, one on the Isle Sainte- Margeurite. It was a great feeling being ushered to the front row on every occasion. On the front of the building of the Baelen's apartment was emblazoned Napoleon III. He had lived there, it was said, with his mistresses. Again while there I was to back into a car, this time the Jaguar of a Frenchman. Again more convivial drinks *chez-lui* followed to settle the affair.

On our second visit to Cannes, Eliane invited us to lunch halfway through at their villa in St Tropez. She said rather shyly did I mind meeting a Princess? I said not at all. So I was sat at table between Tatiana Fruchaud and another delightful lady who I understood lived in a large chateau in Alsace where they kept monkeys. Rather overwhelmed by my company I caused considerable mirth among the family, when, not thinking, I continued to cut up the rind of my melon and eat it. It turned out Tatiana was the granddaughter of King Constantine of Greece and also very interestingly a direct descendant of Napoleon Bonaparte. On a visit to Ajaccio, Corsica (having had supper with the Fruchauds in Paris on the way), Mary and I were to see Tatiana's name at the bottom of the Napoleonic family tree on the wall of Bonaparte's birthplace. A friendly relationship started. By amazing coincidence we had mutual friends, Clifford and Diane Russell. They had already told us about meeting Tatiana and her grandfather on the beach at St Tropez. Tatiana's husband John – his family preferred the English spelling – was a cardiologist. Later, while in Paris, he took me round his hospital.

I have to say Tatiana was not my only contact with royalty. I have to admit to having bumped bottoms with a very willing now Queen of Norway. It happened at the country club at Thorpeness. Mary and I were invited there by her cousin Tim Ruane and his Norwegian wife Tone who had with them Tone's university friend Sonia. At the time she was sheltering from the publicity around the then Prince Harald's proposition to marry her. Like our Prince William, they had all met at university. When it came to my turn to invite Sonia to dance it was Boomps-a-daisy. For those not acquainted with the dance it starts with bumping bottoms once then twice and finally three times. Sonia certainly seemed to enjoy it as much as I did. The marriage took place and now Harald has succeeded his father.

# The Last Decade

Two exciting events happened in this time. First, learning and utilising two forms of complementary medicine; second, taking a three-month sabbatical in India and Sri Lanka.

## Hypnotherapy

I had seen introductory courses in hypnotherapy advertised for some time in the BMJ and thought this to be such an exciting thing to try. So in December 1979 I went on my first course. Little did I realise what a profound change it would make on my medical practice. I had my first lesson in how to induce hypnosis. That evening I tried it out on some of the family staying with my mother-in-law, just up the hill from the Whittington Hospital where the course took place. All cooperated except Mary who giggled. I felt a second course in February was needed before I started to use it on patients.

Complementary medicine was not in vogue then. For this first occasion I arranged a special session at the end of a surgery for a patient suffering from simple anxiety. I told my receptionist that I was not to be interrupted by any phone calls then. Yes otherwise I did allow patients to call me anytime. I held the induction script in my hand. The patient is soon asked to close their eyes, so one can't be seen reading, and I let go. I was elated and relieved to see at the end how well the patient responded and relaxed. From then on, I began to use hypnotherapy on more and more patients, using it at the drop of a hat as I became more familiar with it. As any GP knows, anxiety is present in so many of our patients, whether on its own or in association with conditions such as asthma, angina, cancer, fear of operations (or even doctors in white coats).

"I haven't felt so relaxed for years. Why haven't I done this before?" said many patients. For me I felt a positive delight in seeing an anxious patient I could help so simply, when before I was filled with dread. Previously I could only reach for my pad to prescribe tranquillisers.

About hypnotherapy, I have to say I think it has an unfortunate connotation and association with stage hypnotherapists. I wish it could be given another name. It is really just a method of relaxation that is second to none. There are many other ways of relaxing such as meditation, mindfulness and yoga, – in my opinion not so easy to learn or to produce such a profound effect.

Prince William has mentioned in public that he used daily meditation, which came in for a certain amount of criticism. It would be impossible for him to admit to practising self-hypnosis or, God forbid, to consulting a hypnotherapist such is the belief that he would admit in that way to having his mind dangerously influenced. Now rather stop press his wife the Duchess of Cambridge has let it be known she used hypnobirthing for her three pregnancies. What a sensible lady. Let us hope many will follow in her footsteps.

However, all hypnosis is really self-hypnosis. The therapist just aids the patient, and no-one can do anything against their will. Knowing the method, he or she can then continue to practise on their own. I did use tapes later.

It is not time consuming for the GP: quite the opposite. To illustrate – a postman repeatedly came to me suffering from recurrent attacks of asthma, stress-related, that were about to cause him to lose his job. Teaching him self-hypnosis in one session, I didn't see him again for another year.

Another patient with tension headaches had one session all within a ten- to fifteen-minute appointment. Seen again for follow up a few weeks later, the headaches had improved while practising his daily relaxation. He said he didn't require a further lesson from me. He knew how to do it. His wife told me he continued to use his relaxation in breaks in his tractor cab. Years later, having not seen him in the interval, I heard that he had used his relaxation while others panicked, waiting for his arm trapped in a conveyor belt to be amputated.

One group of patients most satisfying to help in my last ten years were my expectant mothers. At their antenatal visits while on the couch I gave them a brief induction for them to continue both before and then during labour in the first stage, and between contractions in the second. Most did very well. One, who had put off having a second baby for ten years after a bad experience in her first, arrived at Ipswich to be told she was hardly in labour as she was so relaxed. However, they said she had better stay at hospital as she was such a long way from home. The baby arrived half an hour later. Another mother had her delivery at home before she could get on her way to hospital after delaying when her midwife neighbour told her she was too relaxed to be in labour. It came minutes later.

Another mother impressed me when after being taught self-hypnosis at her ante-natal visits, her labour in the second stage of pushing became prolonged and difficult due to the presentation of the baby, an *occipital-posterior*. However, she stayed relaxed. I was present but not utilising any further therapy. When she delivered, I commiserated about the length; but her comment was, "I couldn't have done it if I hadn't been in your garden."(She was visualising her preferred picture that I had given. Many mothers like the idea of waves.)

There are so many occasions when an ability to induce relaxation can be utilised. After diagnosing a patient with a recent bout of chest pain to be suffering from a coronary thrombosis and needing admission to hospital, I was able to help him relax by simply asking him about a pleasant memory, in his case a South Pacific island when a marine. Using that slow rhythmical voice, asking him to breathe in and out slowly and visualising his scene, he was soon away. He said he only came to as he was being wheeled along the corridors at hospital.

Another occasion arriving at a motorcyclist lying on the side of the road with a compound fracture of his femur, his thigh bone sticking through his skin, before any ambulance arrived I simply asked him his name and then said, "Tommy close your eyes and think of something nice." He closed his eyes, a smile came across his face and he said, "Yes, it is nice but something rather naughty!" He was away. A woman came to me very anxious the day before going into hospital for a hysterectomy. I gave her a quick lesson in self-hypnosis. She told me afterwards that a day or two after the operation she lay on her bed and thought she would put into practice what I had taught her. The next moment the alarm was raised, and nurses came rushing around to resuscitate her. After explaining to them she was only doing her relaxation she was told, "Please warn them next time."

Our local prison Blundeston asked me to help one of their inmates with hypnotherapy for his trouble with sleeping. My location to see the prisoner was the infirmary. My only problem was the prison officer, standing outside the door, would intrude now and again to make sure all was well. I had always thought if I was incarcerated in a cell I would use my self hypnosis to visualise being on some far away shore. My prisoner a young Irishman responded quite well. Being a catholic I afterwards sent him a rosary. Saying the beads can be one sure way of nodding off. I often wondered if it was let through the censor.

Dying can be an anxious time for some. That said I found the most worried patients were often those who had nothing wrong with them but came fearing the worst. Once diagnosis was made of a terminal illness, most became resigned to it. But for those who were anxious I found that teaching self-hypnosis was very calming. I would help them to visualise a garden, which they could equate with paradise if they liked. I can always remember a patient with advanced lung cancer being very anxious then becoming quite calm in this way to the end.

Where hypnotherapy can be helpful in the hands of a trained therapist, other than for simple relaxation, is for more complex mental problems, such as post-traumatic stress disorder (PTSD) and severe phobias. This does need more time, something I was so pleased to be able to do after my retirement. (I had learnt the basics in my last ten years in practice.)

The point is illustrated by my treatment of a 13-year-old girl, a patient of a partner on holiday, who came to me with more complex problems in the last week before my retirement. I think I can say without this chance use of hypnotherapy she might well have been suffering for life. She was already being investigated by a gastroenterologist for abdominal pains. These had occurred all her life but had worsened in the previous seven months to the extent that she was even fearful to visit her grandmother, let alone go to school. I can say after six sessions she became a new person. Back at school her mother said she was even helping other pupils with anxiety, using the methods I had taught her. Living in the same district I can see how life has continued to be satisfactory for her since. The gastroenterologist in a letter did in fact give me somewhat grudging acknowledgement.

Practising hypnotherapy did put me in demand for giving talks on the subject. The Southwold WI was one to ask me. I remember well one lady in the third row asking me to speak up when I was using my soft voice. The Young Farmers were particularly keen to have me. First at Halesworth, where I had a problem overcoming the giggles of the girlfriends, when starting an induction demonstration, but managed it in the end. Loddon Young Farmers asked me twice. They so liked it. But was it a shortage of speakers or my fee being just a G&T beforehand?

I later gave a talk at a conference of the Franco-Britannique Medical Society held at Herstmonceux Castle, Sussex. I had always wanted to give an induction in French. To demonstrate the power of suggestion I asked them to close their eyes with both arms held out in front, one with hands facing up to hold a heavy dictionary, on the other arm three helium balloons coloured, *bleu, blanc, rouge,* tugging at the wrist. Then a bible on the dictionary – it weighs; more balloons- it pulls. Asked at the end to open their eyes it was a delight to see the French President in front of me, his arms at all angles, bursting into laughter.

My most attentive of followers taking an interest in hypnotherapy at the conference was a party of medical students and their charming lady teacher from Nantes. We corresponded for a while afterwards. I was rather taken by the report of one of the girl students in the society journal, in her best English – "We did enjoy the conference at Herstmonceux Castle, and we were even *hypnosed* by Doctor Hopkins." The conferences were also the means to get to know a *très aimable* couple the Blanvillains. As with *nos amis* at Cannes we have continued to communicate in their own language on the phone at Christmas ever since. Sadly both husbands have since died.

# Acupuncture

It was after using hypnotherapy for five years that I became interested in and started treating patients with acupuncture. This happened at a day conference in London on Holistic Medicine that had Prince Charles as its patron. In a large hall were spread out tables with all the complementary therapies you could imagine... reflexology, colour therapy, the lot. After a general talk we were assigned to the different tables. I was assigned to one of the few doctors there who was dealing with acupuncture. He impressed me by saying his own sinusitis was only cured by acupuncture after years of unsuccessful conventional treatment. Fired by this, I went on a day course at Cambridge organised by the British Medical Acupuncture Society. Heading it was a doctor wearing my old school tie. Given a lot of dos and don'ts and a practice with needles on each other, we were encouraged to start right away. I was to meet up with the fellow I had needled in the gents at another meeting of the hypnotherapy society in Cambridge a week later; on asking me if I remembered him, he rolled up his sleeve to show a large bruise.

It was only after another day course in acupuncture at the Homeopathic Hospital in London that I felt courageous enough to start on one of my patients. It was a man with low back pain. I didn't mention acupuncture to him, as complementary medicine was not as yet popularised. I just said I was going to put a needle in his back. Very soon I felt comfortable enough to use the term. With a separate examination room, it was easy to put a patient on the couch there, insert the needles and leave them while seeing another patient next door.

Did it work? I was to see some amazing results. A retired lady almoner sent to me by the physiotherapist as she felt she could do no more for her, arrived in severe pain hardly able to walk. She was not even able to turn over completely on the couch. After treatment she stood up with the pain much relieved, walking normally and saying, "I am now going off for a swim." A man on holiday came in bitterly complaining of severe pain in his upper arm, wearing a sling and asking for stronger painkillers than his doctor had given him. When I applied acupuncture needles to the area a smile came over his face. He left off his sling and walked out pain-free to the amazement of his wife in the waiting room. Feedback came from a patient who had met this fellow at the Red Lion one day in a sling and the next using the same arm to raise a pint, saying he had had the wonders of acupuncture from a local doctor. My landlord came in with postherpetic neuralgia saying, "If man can get to the moon, why can't they relieve his pain?" I told him there was a therapy 2000 years old that could be tried, called acupuncture. Much to his amazement and mine, (as I had been told on one of my courses it had little effect for this particular pain), it worked on him with complete success. However, I was somewhat disillusioned at an acupuncture conference at Cheltenham where a doctor read a paper on a trial he had made, comparing acupuncture with sham acupuncture. The result was the same: about 30% benefit in both. But if it's only the place-bo effect, 30% is worth it after all.

At this stage I was open to give anything a trial to see if it could be of benefit. I tried reflexology one morning on Mary for her to have her best round of golf that day. But I didn't see myself pressing the soles of any of my patients. Neuro-linguistic Programming (NLP) as an addition to hypno-therapy started in the 1990s and had its enthusiasts. I tried and discarded a lot of it as being far-fetched but found some of it, particularly the Swish, helpful. The Swish is a very simple mental exercise to use. It consists of, with eyes closed, visualising the scene in front of you that is bothering, then changing the picture as in a slide show, with yourself in it looking relaxed and happy, and then to open your eyes. This is all repeated up to ten times. I tried it in my bath one morning for my fear of speech making. Without thinking, that evening at a doctor's conference in a full hall, I found myself speaking without a qualm when the audience was asked to ask questions at the end. Thinking about or using these alternative therapies did give me an added interest and excitement as well as benefit to the ordinary practice of medicine.

# India and Sri Lanka

For many years I had been thinking of having a break to practise in the third world. Previously an attempt to effect an exchange with a practitioner in the then Rhodesia had come to nothing. Then in 1986 I heard of an organisation, Action Health 2000 based at Cambridge, run by a Dr Mukesh, himself of Indian origin. He was sending health workers to India and Africa.

After an interview I was chosen to be attached to a small children's hospital in the temple city of Madurai in Tamil Nadu State, South India. The name Madurai, pronounced 'Maduray', sounded quite magical to me. I think it helped to show my keenness by having been on a week's course at the Greenwich Hospital the previous year with a surgeon who went once a year to the wilds of South East Asia to give surgical help. He taught us how to trephine on the skull and much more. We all had a go at operating, myself to repair a hernia.

Sabbaticals for up to a year were encouraged by the NHS at that time to enlarge one's ability to practise. Locums were paid for. On a second attempt at making a case I was accepted, as also the consent of my partners, and as locum my recently retired partner Graham Bracewell.

So on 4th January 1987 I set off from London Airport, arriving at Madurai three days later. It included a 24-hour train journey from Bombay to Bangalore, a night there, before a final flight to Madurai. Mary had opted to only join me after my first month. Luckily my sister Rosemary was coming to visit the Boys' Town of Joe Homan 20 miles away from Madurai at just that time, so they journeyed out together.

I was very comfortably lodged in a villa in a smart suburb of Madurai with a party comprising ophthalmologists, nurses, medical students, general helpers and wives. In charge, very much like a house mother, was Mrs Janaki, sister of Dr Venkataswamy. It was he who had invited me. He had founded a large eye hospital the Aravind many years before, where many cases of Xerophthalmia were resulting from poor health and malnutrition in childhood. This made him decide to help the young by opening an adjoining children's hospital two years before my arrival. He already had ophthalmologists from Britain and the USA to advise him at the Aravind. Now he wanted advice for childcare from a British GP (I kept a daily diary during my stay, now printed).

On arrival I was taken straight away to meet Dr Venkataswamy at the Aravind. After a most friendly meeting he immediately invited me to join a meeting of 5–6 of the hospital doctors discussing the future Eye Camps held for treating cataracts at places all over Tamil Nadu. All Indians, it was interesting to find, they spoke in English. Dr V saw me again the next morning to tell me his plan of action for me: namely in the next two weeks to visit and study all the local services and projects. He called me an expert in community medicine, which was very reassuring.

I went on to visit the children's hospital nearby to be introduced to the doctors, the matron, nurses and receptionists, all dressed in their white saris. Daily outpatients were held there and available were ten or so beds for in-patients, some of them private. The three doctors were all of different religions, Hindu, Moslem and Christian (RC) which I was told was by chance – Mumtaz and Kanchara both ladies, and Paul Raj. Despite the fact I was supposed to be advising them, they could not have been more welcoming. They didn't need it. The main inhibiting factor as I was to discover was lack of funds for medicine and equipment. The two other functions of the hospital were to visit the local slum of Madurai and to hold 2–3 times a week 'camps' (clinics) at villages in the countryside around. It was there that I could at least play some active part.

A chance to visit a slum came immediately, as Linda, the attached nurse from Action Health 2000, was about to visit the Nehrujipuram slum on the other side of the Vaigai river flowing nearby. The Tamil social worker

Sandra made the other one of the party. The main object of the visit was to follow up some babies to weigh them. At one spot with a small tree having a branch for the weighing machine, I tie it on with a clove hitch, my one big action of the day.

The slum, consisting of 350 largely thatched roofed one room homes for cooking, eating and sleeping, lay in neat rows sloping down to the river. A drain ran in front with standpipes for washing at frequent intervals and a pipe for drinking at one end only. It must have been a government construction, as its name suggested, under or in memory of Nehru.

I had my first chance of practising my Tamil on a bunch of kids following us around. *"E Peri Hopkins, enga peri ennouga?"* – "My name is Hopkins what is yours?" One bright lad answered "Mark" and then stayed with us until we reached the main road.

My first experience of a children's camp came the next day. It took the usual routine. A minibus filled up outside the children's hospital at 1.00pm with a doctor, two nurses, nutritionists, boxes of medicines and on this occasion a British medical student (Richard), a visiting American (Danny) and me. The camp was being held in a village 24 km from Madurai and was taking place as usual in a school building. Publicity and organisation of the children's hospital was done by a local group who asked the hospital to come. This happened once in three months to give the children a check-up and treat as necessary. In the meantime, if they needed help they could see a local doctor for five rupees plus medicine. Doctors were very thin on the ground – only 10% of doctors being in the country for the majority of the Indian population.

The clinic was 2.00pm–5.00pm. On this occasion we saw 125 children – about average. I sat and watched with Dr Kanchova. Mothers, occasionally fathers, brought the children in. The common complaints were upper respiratory tract infections; scabies (treated with sulphur ointment); dysentery (with Furazolidine); worm infection (with Piperazine); Xerophthalmia (treated with Vitamin A liquid on two days running plus advice from the nutritional nurse). Various skin complaints were treated. A small abscess on the back was drained, with a scalpel, by the expert nurse. All were given vitamin C or B tablets as some medicine must be given to all to entice them to come. Everything was free. With the exception of the really sick ones, the children all looked very happy and always milled around and gave us a great send off at the end.

An important part of some children's treatment was to deal with their nutritional state. A Nutritional Centre had been set up for this in 1971 where the children could stay for 3–6 weeks, living in a row of one room compartments with cooking facilities included. Support was often given by a sister not much older than themselves, as mothers had to continue to work. A small kitchen garden at the end showed the families how to grow the necessary vegetables high in vitamin K to prevent Xerophthalmia.

My usual routine for the first two weeks was just to sit and watch, either at the hospital or at the camps. All three doctors were very chatty. They could see I was very keen to learn Tamil and helped me. There was time at the hospital as it was often not very busy. I was dying to get started and lend a hand but felt even with an interpreter I must at least have a smattering of the language.

I had made a beginning studying with leaflets from the School of Oriental and African Studies in the weeks before coming to India. Pronunciation having to convert from one script to another can make things difficult, as I was soon to find out.

At a camp two weeks after my arrival I felt I was up to it even without an interpreter but was immediately in trouble. I said to a boy of about six, *"Sutte payen"*, thinking it meant 'strong boy'. He looked blank and a bit dismayed. After he left, I discovered from the Tamil nurses that my pronunciation of *'sutte'* with tongue forward meant 'dead boy'... No wonder! For 'strong' the point of the tongue must be back. Truly a tongue-twisting language.

Although I was dying to be involved in a more hands-on position, I began to realise that Dr V wanted me there mainly to observe, then give my general advice, give talks to the doctors and health visitors, teach the nurses and write reports to him. Within a week of my arrival, as part of an ophthalmic conference for doctors from all over India and of Indian origin from USA, a buffet supper was held at night on the roof of the Avarind Hospital. The air was balmy with a full moon above. The lights of the city including those on the "Gopuram" towers of the famous Meenakshi Temple could be seen in the distance. In my shirtsleeves I felt how wonderful it was to be out there while England was shivering in a great freeze with even Heathrow airport being out of action for a day.

Two days later came *Pongal Day*, always kept rather like Christmas combined with Harvest Festival. It was held particularly in Tamil Nadu every year around the 14th January, lasting up to four days. Sheaves of sugar canes lined the streets in the centre of Madurai like Christmas trees. Greetings *"Pongal Waterkal"* (Happy Pongol) were given and cards exchanged. I gave one to the children's hospital which I continued to do a year or two after I left.

The first evening Mrs Janiki arranged a minibus to take all of us to a concert of Indian music at the Music Theatre. Then again, on the second day of Pongol "for the animals", when most of the cows have their horns painted, heads bedecked with flowers and bodies painted, we were taken to attend a celebration at a farmhouse in the country. Gaily dressed dancers moving with objects such as flowerpots balanced on their heads, all accompanied by the flutes and banging of drums, performed in front of us in a farmyard. There were several scenes with fire. In one bizarre dance, four small boys lay on the floor with bananas sticking out of the top of their trousers. Lady dancers, blindfolded, twirling large knives sliced the bananas up. We finished with a feast on banana leaves but none to eat.

## The Eye Camp

The next morning a team of four Aravind doctors with nurses and equipment loaded up a minibus to travel the 100 miles or so to Madras (now known as Chennai) to set up an eye camp. Danny, the medical student Richard and I accompanied them. This took place in an orphanage. Preparation and screening of 3–400 people started. Organisation was helped by an interdenominational religious group whose leader is Sri Sai Baba, whom they regard as divine and can work miracles such as producing rings and watches in his hand from nowhere. His main motive is love and helping others, hence organising free eye camps.

Finishing the preparations by 3.00pm, I took a rickshaw bicycle to visit St Thome Cathedral where St Thomas the Apostle is buried. Many people don't realise that Christianity reached South India when Britons were still wearing woad. England had to wait for St Augustine in the 6th Century. I also visited St Mary's Anglican Church where there were many memorials to the British dead, too many it seemed at an early age. I returned to St Thome for the Saturday evening mass. Walking back to our hotel afterwards I became very lost and panicky in the mass of streets. I hadn't taken down the name of our hotel or its address. But I did make it in the end, and with Danny we finished the day with a visit to a nearby temple.

Woken next morning at 6.30am, we arrived at the orphanage to find the cataract operations well underway. They had started at 4.30am to beat the heat and had already done 50 cases.

Patients were lined up on chairs outside the 'theatre' to have nerve blocks installed to the eye. They were then transferred into the large hall to sit watching others operated on while waiting their turn. The surgeons, now increased to five, operated along a row of tables. Nurses stood by in attendance. All was very quiet and calm. Operating time for the quickest surgeon was four minutes, the total of 142 cataract operations being done by 8.30am. The patients were to stay a few more days looked after by a small staff. The team quickly packed up and we were on our way back to the Aravind.

## Patchamael's Village

Two weeks later I was invited by an Indian called Patchamael to visit his village Kamatchipuram, a four-hour bus journey away. I had met Patchaemael, a most genial and cheerful man, at my orientation day at the headquarters of Action Health 2000, Cambridge while he was visiting there. He wanted me to see for myself how he had set up a Health Centre in his village one and a half years previously. He started the centre with a nurse from AH 2000 but now had an Indian nurse. He was a farmer's son who decided he must do some good for his village. A particularly interesting event I took part in was a bi-annual meeting of CENDECT (Centre for Development and Communication Trust), started by Patchamael in 1983, four years before, as a means of helping the *harigans* (outcasts) and the landless in the village.

Taking place in the open under the shade of a tree, the other members came from Madras and Delhi and other parts of Tamil Nadu. After talking about local problems such as sinking a well for a family whose mother had committed suicide – a dowry death and another well for the harigans-the meeting became more political. The main object was to organise the harigans to act for themselves. My question: "Are they accused of being communists?" Answer – by politicians – "Yes." One member mentions that in Kerala the communist government in power put a ceiling on the amount of land anyone could have, redistributing it to the landless. These then kept their workers on low wages, became part of the landed class and voted the communists out. The meeting ended with them saying they must always keep the poor in mind. Certainly not all Indians are only interested in making themselves rich regardless of the poor.

I was to see for myself over the weekend what life was like in an ordinary Indian village. I slept on the floor in the village school with no lavatory or washing facilities and had meals off banana leaves without utensils. I had already seen the children at Madurai lining up in the gutter in front of their school to relieve themselves. As I wandered around, I felt I was an object of interest. They rarely saw a westerner. Patchamael and his wife were very sweet, she presenting me with two giraffes made at her workshop. I was able later to give them to a delighted child in a slum who, as all others, had not a single toy.

## Mary Arrives

Mary arrived to join me on 4th February looking beautiful with a new shorter haircut. She was soon introduced round the guest house and we went on to visit the children's hospital. We then visited the Government Hospital to see how the ordinary Indians are treated. The main wards were very grubby but the maternity wing immaculate. We saw four children in recovery from tetanus (usually 90% mortality) and ten with polio,

*Our transport on the Backwaters, Kerala.*

*Mary, Anthony, Pat and our chauffeur, Seliya, at the Royal Botanic Gardens, Kandy.*

*The 'Inevitable Photograph' – Mary in front of the Taj Mahal.*

*On an elephant at the roadside to Kandy.*

David Porter M.P.

HOUSE OF COMMONS
LONDON SW1A 0AA

6th April 1990.

Dear Dr Hopkins

     I was sorry to receive your letter of 27th March and to learn of your early retirement from the practice.

     I remember well your warnings from previous correspondence but I am still sorry you have taken the view that you have.

     I am grateful for your keeping me informed of the reasons for your stand, which will certainly assist me in considering my view on the effectiveness of the new contracts and other parts of the Health Service reforms.

Yours sincerely

David Porter

Dr. C.J. Hopkins,
83 High Street,
Southwold, IP18 6DS.

*A letter from David Porter MP on my resignation from practice.*

*The family ... now four children.*

*In the sea opposite 10 North Parade.*
*The log had floated down to Southwold as a result of coastal erosion at Benacre.*

*On the front at North Parade, Southwold.*
*Mary with Frances and Tina.*

*Mary in St John's Wood, London*
*just before coming to Southwold.*

*Frances, Tina and James on the beach in front of our house.*
*Inset: William with our dog, Dusty.*

*On my horse, Harlequin, at Hunter Trials.*

*Southwold Rugby Team opening season 1964. Peter Kemsley (Captain) kneeling in the centre with the ball. I am behind him to the left. David Mitchell is a further two to the left from me and Bernard Segrave-Daly is immediately to the right of the church tower.*

*Ford House in the snow.*

*Friends enjoying a glass of Pimms at Ford House after tennis. John Veitch, on the left, chatting to Barbara Wheeler. Beyond, his wife talking to Mary and John Holmes in the centre and, on the right, John Hashim deep in discussion with Jim Wheeler.*

*The cousins ... the Jacques, the Chilcotts and the Hopkins (missing five McDowells).*

*The next generation! The thirteen grandchildren.*

illnesses no longer (or rarely) seen in the UK. We went on to visit the adjoining Nutritional Centre. It was here that Mary and two other helpers later set up a play group with picture books, painting and bat and ball. I gave a talk there to a group of health visitors about the NHS. One man asked me, "Do you not favour private patients?"

## British Organisations

In our stay at Mandurai we took the opportunity to visit three centres in the Tamil Nadu state for the poor and needy organised by Britishers, two from East Anglia. The first while my sister Rosemary was there was Joe Homan's Boys' Town. Joe had been a lay brother of the De La Salle order at St Joseph's College, Ipswich. He taught Michael and Richard Jellicoe, the grandsons of the owner of the ladies fashion shop in Queen St Southwold, Mrs Mella Nicholls. Emigrating to India, Joe was disturbed by seeing young Indian boys just hanging around railway stations. To help them he started up his first Boys' Town to house, educate and train them to find work. Joe had explained all this in a talk at Queen's Street that enthralled Mary and me.

We reached the nearby town of Tiramangalum by bus and finally by rickshaw bicycle out to Joe Homan's. Set in the country it comprised five boys' houses with fifteen boys in each house aged ten to fifteen years old. Apart from Joe all the staff were Indian. Michael Jellicoe had been attached there. Also separate across the fields was a Girls' Town started later by Joe. The fields looked very dry and parched although now only February.

The next centre we visited under the name of 'Reaching the Unreached' (RTU) was situated some 50 miles to the west of Madurai in the foothills of the Ghats mountains. We had heard of it from Michael Jellicoe who transferred there from Joe to stay another year. It was again started and run by a De La Salle Brother, Br James Kingston. We were even more impressed by his set up. Also, out in the country, he built and housed orphaned children in family groups, mothered by widows he had taken in. From this caring base the children could attend local schools and be prepared in the end to go out into the world to make a living.

He organised workshops, in particular one producing Batik cloths.

There was also a health centre with a visiting doctor. On our second visit to the RTU we arrived in time for the drama of a man brought in on a bed at the back of a truck. He had fallen down a dry well and fractured his femur. On making my way through the large crowd to reach him, an old woman (presumably his mother) prostrated herself before me and kissed the ground. Br James, a water diviner, was a great benefactor to the surrounding district by sinking much needed wells.

Olive Jeffries was the third British-organised health project we visited, situated just outside Madurai. Olive was a remarkable lady. A physiotherapist, she had given up her practice in Colchester in middle age four years previously to come to India and found a health centre. This included a workshop for nursing mothers making dolls to make some sort of living for them.

## Mountain Breaks

During our stay Mary and I had two most enjoyable weekend breaks at resorts in the Ghats mountains. The first was the Periyar game reserve where the few remaining tigers still existed. None showed up in a long morning walk through the rain forest guided by a young Indian boy, who being over the border in Kerala State I couldn't communicate with in Tamil. We saw many monkeys up in the trees and a herd of wild elephants with their young.

The other resort, Kodaicanal, was more sophisticated with a more luxurious hotel on the edge of a beautiful lake and a boarding school. The Rifkins, Danny's family at the guest house, had a daughter there. The hotel was full of honeymooners chatting vigorously. Obviously arranged marriages, it was their first chance of being alone. The cool atmosphere of both resorts made a pleasant change from the hot plains.

We took the hair-raising bus back down to the plain lasting all of one-and-three-quarter-hours, screeching round every bend as if in a race. At the bottom we dropped off to catch another bus to stay a night at "Reaching the Unreached" – our second visit to see the drama of the man who fell down the well. On the final bus journey back to Madurai, having a long conversation with a man in pigeon Tamil, he asked me "Is your God Jesus?"

# Getting About in Madurai

There was also much to visit in Madurai itself. In particular there was the famous Meenakshi Temple, one of the largest in India. Spread over 14 acres it comprised numerous courtyards, shrines, weird sculptures and the large golden lotus sacred pool. Towering above were the 14 gopurams (towers). At the entrance you deposited your shoes in exchange for slippers, hoping you will get yours back again. Most fascinating was the elephant holding out its trunk for a coin and then blessing you on the forehead with its hot breath. We visited the temple many times.

On a less cultural level, on several evenings to have a drink we called on the two quite well-appointed hotels on the outskirts of Madurai just beyond us, the Panyon and Ashok. On one occasion we met staying at the Panyon Dr John Ryder Richardson, a GP at Saxmundham, with his wife Eleanor. They were in the middle of a tour round India in an inter-denominational Christian group led by the Dean of Chester. Another time after drinks at the Ashok with four girls from the Guest House we decided to have a bicycle rickshaw race back. The rickshaw wallahs entered into the spirit of it despite one of the girl pairs being definitely on the large size. With her partner they tried a short cut in the darkness but lost their way. Our man got right ahead but then halted short of the guest house and Mary and I were pipped at the post.

Having met his sister at Reaching the Unreached we got an invitation to tea at his residence by the Catholic Archbishop of Madurai. It was Ash Wednesday and seeing a very large spread on the drawing room table I asked if it was right for that day. The Archbishop with a beaming mischievous smile that put us in mind of the good Archbishop Tutu of South Africa reassured us: "I give you dispensation." We had a good discussion about the problem of Christians in some militant Hindu areas mostly in the North. Asking his opinion on Family Planning he said it was difficult. He was not in complete accord with the Pope.

On our last day we visited the Madurai Country Club. As with all British abroad who have to keep up their sporting facilities even in a hot climate, it was founded by the once British-owned Coats Factory. It included tennis courts, a swimming pool and attractive clubhouse. We were soon swimming followed by drinks at the bar.

## The Guest House

There was plenty of jollification with the party in the guest house itself. Conversation round the table at mealtimes was always lively. Serving us was Pandy, once in the service of a British Colonel. I was very chuffed to hear from someone who followed me that Pandy described me as the one who laughed a lot. The good Mrs Janiki, presiding over us, often joined in the talk. The food was European with an Indian flavour. I really enjoyed curry at first, in particular the curried crab, but began to tire of the curry towards the end. I especially didn't care for dahl at breakfast.

On many evenings after supper we sat up in the dark under the stars on the roof terrace drinking beer. This was the only alcohol you could buy in the shops. Wine of an Indian origin was on offer at hotels but not that good. On one evening the American Corrie Rifkin organised the Aravind Guest House Follies. I was MC, my one act to sing nursery rhymes with two-year-old Omar, Corrie's son. With numerous young children, Indian and the Rifkins, we had Oranges and Lemons, Here We Go Gathering Nuts in May and the Hoki Coki, much enjoyed by all. The several Indian young present especially enjoyed the finale singsong that I led – Clementine, Camp Down Races and Cockles and Mussels. After supper Janiki wanted to see us dance, when I taught her niece Kalpona, a medical student, the waltz.

Another evening Joe Homan rode over for dinner on his motorbike with Rosemary as his pillion. He gave us a long account of his Boy's Town. One interesting fact was that he found the local doctors very good and affordable for the poor and found not the same need to run clinics himself.

## More at the Camps and Clinics

All these happenings in the evenings and weekends didn't stop me attending the daily Hospital Outpatients and twice weekly Village Camps. I came to know the friendly doctors and nurses and social workers better and better. Dr Shandra, who was about to have an arranged marriage, asked if we couldn't stay on longer to attend it. She was quite happy with the arrangement although only having met her future husband, never alone, for one hour on two occasions.

When my colleagues heard that I did acupuncture I was asked to bring my needles to the clinic. The opportunity came to use them on a young boy with headaches. The mother was agreeable, the boy not so keen. I used the standard treatment I was taught – a needle between each big toe and the next. At least no harm was done as she very pleasantly asked after me when she saw Dr Michael Dickson, a GP from Halesworth on his tour at Madurai a year later. My two talks to the doctors ordered by Dr V were a bit embarrassing for fear of seeming to talk down to them, but they always took it well.

One of the camps nearly turned into a riot. Very noisy children crammed themselves into the schoolroom where Dr Mumtaz and I were seeing patients. At one time for some reason Mumtaz above the din shouted, "I feel like dancing!" But then she had had enough of it and ordered the lot out. The Tamil nurses were very devout Hindus and sometimes at the end of a camp we went out of our way to visit a shrine. At one I was garlanded by a priest. In a minibus the young nurses couldn't tolerate a man sharing a bench with them. If you did, they immediately removed themselves.

## The Indian Finale

Our time at Madurai was coming to an end. It was our plan to move on to Sri Lanka and then Kerala on the west side of South India, finally ending up at Delhi. Just before leaving we managed to find time to visit Chellem who had fallen down the well. He was now in the Government Hospital, his fractured femur in traction, his wife sitting by him. I secreted 100 rupees into a packet with biscuits and chocolate. He avoided saying anything with patients around but looked grateful with his eyes as he clasped my hand.

We said farewell to Dr V in his office. He thanked us with a presentation of a five metal Tandur plate. (Was this as much for Mary's help with the floral decoration at the hospital and guest house and her organising the playgroup at the nutritional centre as for me?) We made our farewells at the Children's Hospital and guest house before the Aravind Superintendant Tulsi took us to the express bus for Tiruchirippalli (Trichy), a three-hour journey to the North. We needed the airport there to take us on to Colombo.

My remarks in the Guest House visitors' book said it all ...

*"As we come to the end of our time here, I would first like to thank Janiki and her staff for the great hospitality they have shown us. Secondly to Dr V, our friendly and good humoured task master for his encouragement and support. Thirdly to the doctors, nurses and social workers at the children's hospital for making us feel so much part of the team. I wish them and Dr Lakshmi well in the big task ahead. Finally, to all our fellow guests for their wonderful company and the happy times we have had together."*

## Tiruchirippalli (Trichy)

Our one evening and night at Trichy turned out to be one of the most stirring and exciting in the whole of our time on the Indian subcontinent. No doubt the prospect of visiting another country added to it. Extracts from my diary sum it up:

*Arrive at the pleasant Aristo Hotel set in its own gardens. Our room with shower and WC costs just £7.50 for the two of us. Rickshaw taxi to the Rock Fort Temple – interesting town, its last part through narrow streets of the bazaar. Climb up the steps inside the rock until we emerge by the temple at the top. Magnificent views over the Couvery River where the British fought the French. Out again in a lovely evening by taxi to the Sri Ranganathasway Temple, reputed to be the largest in India.*

*Surrounded by seven concentric walls it has twenty-one Gopurams. Our driver takes us through the archway of the three outer walls with spaces for bazaars on either side of the narrow crowd-thronged road until we reach the entrance of the fourth wall where we have to alight. A young man, pleasantly spoken, immediately greets us giving all sorts of information and then offers his services as a guide. We accept for 10 R. Our shoes come off as we enter the first archway. He explains the main temple is dedicated to Vishnu. He describes the other gods – the god for enjoyment, who had 100+ wives and is depicted always playing a pipe. He shows us a wall with carvings of this god and also several full-breasted, narrow-waisted women. We pass through several chambers and out into the courtyards with columns and carvings. He shows a carving of a monkey, which is several imposed on one. We see the hill of 1000 pillars, in fact 980, now used by the government to store rice. We hear drums beating and our guide says we must see the start of the procession. This proves very exciting – Vishnu being carried on a dais around the temple having been brought out from the inner temple supported by poles protruding front and back on the backs of at least 20 priests, bare-chested wearing orange lungis. The procession moves off with drummers beating ahead followed by two carrying flaming torches, the whole company looking very cheerful. We follow until it emerges at the gateway of the fourth wall, where as it is proceeding to go round it we say goodbye to our good and interesting guide paying him 20 rupees. There was our rickshaw wallah still waiting for us in the now darkness. We drive off back to the town under the light of a half moon. In the streets of Trichy, we pass another drum beating procession with a line of girls with floral crowns on their heads. Dinner was outside on the lawn of our hotel in the warmth of the night.*

## Sri Lanka

The flight over the sea from India to Sri Lanka was thrilling. From the front of the aircraft we had good views of the string of islands connecting the two lands and then the swoop down to Colombo airport over forests of palm trees.

Our stay in Sri Lanka was divided into three parts: a hotel on the beach at Negombo just up the coast from Colombo; at the residence of the British High Commissioner John Stewart and his wife Geraldine in Colombo; and finally a tour with our friends Antony and Pat Romer-Grundy round the island. Pat was John's sister. She and Antony ran the Wangford village shop. Pat's mother living with them, I had been at hand when she needed to go into hospital (although not her main doctor) and was present at her death. I had met John on his visits to his mother. Hence with probably a bit of a nudge from Antony we were invited to stay with them. Fortune so often on our side, Pat and Antony were also there at the same time.

Taking us from the airport to Negombo our taxi driver volunteered, "Life was much better under the British!" It was a pretty fishing village on an estuary, the beach with just a sprinkling of houses on it nearby. It was great to be able to dash across the beach from our hotel after hot dusty Madurai into the warm Indian Ocean. We watched the picturesque brown-sailed catamaran fishing boats sailing in and out of the estuary.

In the four days that we were there I was again able to study local medical care. Taking the bus into the village we came across a derelict-looking building with Health Centre on its front in large letters. It also had a small plaque, saying it was erected in 1936 in commemoration of George V's Jubilee. Inside I found a nurse and a man who said it was in use and a doctor would be coming at 3.00pm the following day for a clinic. Afterwards we talked to some fishermen and children, spreading sardine-like fish to dry on mats on the river shore.

At breakfast next day we came across an English couple just arrived. Carol Davies, a producer and broadcaster in the BBC with her partner Denis were now looking for material about Ayurvedic (Traditional Herbal) Medicine. They were about to visit a hospital five miles inland

practising and teaching this therapy. When I mentioned I was also studying the local medical scene they invited us to join them. The hospital had
thirty beds, shortly to increase to 120 beds with 500 students and was
government-supported. Taken round the wards we noticed the patients
seemed to be mainly suffering from neurological or joint problems – hemi-
plegia; Bell's Palsy; gout; a girl of 23 with pain in the wrists; another of 20
in the arm and leg joints. All had tried western medicine to no avail but
were now improving with Ayurvedic. We were shown the herb garden and
the dispensary where mainly liquid medicines were made.

Carol and Denis had been told about an Ayurvedic doctor (Vedamath
Thaya) who was famous for his dermatological skills. He lived off a track
deep in the palm forest. It was getting dusk as we arrived to see a grizzly
bearded old man living with his rather strange daughter. We were told he
had his own special concoction, inherited from his father, that had cured
a cabinet minister after having had no success at Harley Street. This he
was going to pass in turn to his daughter before he died. Carol took a tape
recording as she had already done at the hospital.

The next day we reported to the Negombo Medical Centre to find a
midwife but no doctor. A man, who told us he had been in the RAF in
the war, and later played cricket for Sri Lanka against Len Hutton and
Boycott, took us to find the Doctor Peries, living just next to our hotel.
We found her a most pleasant lady in her forties. She invited me to attend
her maternity clinic next afternoon.

The following morning we visited the Government Hospital in
Negombo. Turning up out of the blue, the hospital staff could not have
been more friendly. On mentioning my interest in children, I was taken to
join Dr Ira's round taking place at that moment. Out of the ordinary, I saw
a two-month-old baby with malaria, a child with Marasmus/Kwashiorkor
from the troubled North and a fisherman's daughter with lead poisoning
from paint. Dr Ira mentioned being quite upset by the British Government
not allowing her to work in England. She couldn't afford just to study.
She said the British would do better letting her work than by sending
millions of pounds to Sri Lanka. I said I would speak to the British High
Commission about her as I was about to stay with him. No doubt she

would be welcomed with open arms nowadays. Having a blocked ear from all my sea bathing, Dr Ira kindly took me to the ENT department where a nurse soon put me at ease.

Dr Peries took us by car to her maternity clinic in the afternoon. A small dilapidated place, it had cobwebs high up on the walls. About twenty mothers were waiting to be seen. I was told a 55% haemoglobin was regarded as satisfactory, which I felt was on the low side. We finished the day with coffee plus a tasty arrack (the local coconut liqueur) in the evening at the Peries' home.

A taxi took us the next day to the British High Commissioner's residence in Colombo. On seeing the high walls and gates our taxi man said, "Are these your friends?" I said, "Just say Hopkins." The gates opened. Pat and Antony Romer-Grundy greeted us warmly. It was sometime before we saw John and Geraldine Stewart. That evening before dinner we had the strongest G&Ts that I have ever had, poured out by Saniya the butler.

Playing bridge with Mary after dinner, John began to warm, commenting on her good play. By way of conversation I asked him if he knew my nephew Dominick Chillcott, then a secretary at the British Embassy at Ankara. John said he was head of the board that passed him into the Diplomatic Services. Dominick in fact succeeded him at Colombo three to four years later.

The next day, a Sunday, we spent at a pleasant club in the country. We sat under palm trees by the side of an inland lagoon where John barbequed the lunch. I tried my hand on a windsurf board, not very skilfully. At one time John excused himself to meet a lady on another table. He explained later she was British living in the North, and this was his way of finding out surreptitiously what was going on there – all very Graham Greeneish! Back in Colombo, John took us in the evening to a Mass in English.

## The Tour of Sri Lanka

John arranged a complimentary car and chauffeur, both supplied by a travel firm, for a tour of the island with Pat and Antony. Our first destination was Kandy. On our way, lying on its side in a shallow stream beside the road was an elephant. I couldn't resist going down to inspect, when a mahout with another elephant came out of the forest opposite. He got my elephant to squat, and putting a sack cloth on it, invited me to climb on. Once up with surprisingly little jerk, the mahout appeared to want rupees to get me down. Seliya our chauffeur came to my rescue and again the amazing sight of a little man saying one word to a huge animal, and I was let down.

Kandy was as attractive as it sounds. On our first evening we visited the Temple of the Tooth where this part of the Buddha is allegedly kept. Taking place was the ceremony of displaying the casket accompanied by orange-robed priests playing drums and pipes. A daunting display followed with walking on fire.

The next day 17th March was Pat's birthday. We celebrated it with a dinner at the Citadel Hotel. Antony, as was his wont, as we went round the island, let it be known his wife was the sister of the British High Commissioner. The manager presented us with a bottle of wine, a birthday cake and a small metal bowl for Pat. The Calypso players serenaded us with Happy Birthday. We had visited the charming Botanical Gardens in the morning with its beautiful trees and flowering shrubs and a fascinating swarm of fruit bats on one of the trees. On returning to our hotel Antony ordered a bottle of Beaujolais. He invited me to share it but I had had quite enough. He then proceeded to drink it all himself with a surprising effect. He started to speak French volubly, joining up with a French party across the room. At all our French circle evenings Antony had hardly opened his mouth. The Beaujolais had obviously *lui délié la langue*.

We moved off next to the mountains to stay at the Hill Club Hotel, 6,100 feet above sea level. Passing by expanses of tea plantations, we stopped off on the way at a tea factory with machinery a century old made in Belfast. The Hill Club Hotel was part of a sporting complex set up in the days of the British with a golf and racecourse. Mary, Antony and I fitted in a round of golf with caddies before dark set in. As we teed off with most of Antony's and my balls going into the rough, small boys came out of the bushes offering to sell us golf balls. They were probably our own. The Club Hotel was still keeping tradition with a men's only bar and ties after 7.00pm.

We reached the south coastal tip, first through more mountains and then over the plains with paddy fields and buffaloes wading in the water. After spending a night there, we went on through Galle, a largish town with much excitement of an inter-schools' cricket match, taking place under the walls of the Dutch Fort. (It was at Galle that two of our grandsons were caught by the Tsunami of 2004 but were amused by seeing turtles swimming up the high street.) We pressed on up the West coast, seeing the fishermen on stilts off the shore, to arrive and finally stay a night at the splendid Triton Hotel. This had its own beach and a swimming pool reaching into the foyer.

Bathing again in the Indian Ocean was a delight. Antony and I joined in a French party to play water polo. Letting on I had played goalkeeper for the victorious London University team in 1948 seemed to impress. A crab race followed. Antony and I bid in an auction and won a crab we named Maggie after our Prime Minister. The French had a François to represent their President. Bets were placed, the race was on. The first crab has to reach the outside of a circle with spectators all around. Maggie sped away but on nearly reaching the line, the Frenchmen in front of her shouted and jumped up and down so much she turned round in the opposite direction. She ended up last.

We had a final night at the residence in Colombo before saying goodbye to Pat, Antony and the Stewarts to return to the beach at Negombo to fill in another night before our flight on to Kerala. As well as more bathing I had an enjoyable trip out to sea in one of the fishermen's catamaran. Sitting out on planks attached to the outrigger, we bowled along at some six knots over the waves.

## Kerala, South West India

Touching down at Trivandrum we took a taxi to Kovalam on the coast to stay at the Ashok Hotel. Built overlooking the sea and situated on a cliff edge, the lift took us down rather than up to our room. I now had my last chance to study the local medical scene. Kerala, although one of the poorest states, had one of India's best health statistics. This consisted of an immunisation rate of 80% compared with 50% for the rest of India, an infant mortality rate of 29 per thousand compared with 110 and life expectancy of 69 years instead of 59. This was put down to its better level of education with a high literacy rate, especially amongst women. This was thought to be due to the higher number of missionary schools in the state, with 30% of the population being Christian, higher than in any other part of India.

A primary health centre I discovered was 4km away at the village of Vizhentam. A taxi took us there to a grubby looking building. After introductions we sat watching a Doctor Abdullah doing a clinic. Patients in a line of men on one side of his desk and women on the other took turns to be seen. No one seemed to mind being overheard. Each patient was given 25-45 seconds in total for a history, examination and prescription on the piece of paper that each brought with them. It was all free, including medicine. Drugs were very limited. The only antibiotic was Penicillin plus a small ration of Ampicillin per month. But people after sterilisation were entitled to other antibiotics. If patients didn't respond to Penicillin, they were referred to the Trivandrum main hospital. Strolling in the evening on the Keralan beach we could see it was much favoured by the hippy type, with several sitting lotus fashion facing out to sea watching the setting sun.

Our next destination was Cochin, 120 miles up the coast. To get there we decided to utilise for a great part a boat on the Backwaters. This consisted of a series of rivers, canals and lagoons just inland and parallel with the coast. Our boat from Quilon formed the local bus service. There were no tourist cruising vessels then. The scenery going along was completely unspoilt, an enchanting world with fishermen in their old crafts, small canoes, larger wooden boats being rowed, or sailed along with a small square light brown sail, palm trees overhanging the banks. We passed three churches. There were many halts. The whole journey would have taken eight and a half hours, so we decided two and a half was enough and arranged for our taxi man to meet us part of the way. Our journey by boat cost us two and a half rupees each – about 25p.

Cochin was another fascinating place. We stayed at the Malabar Hotel with its garden frontage onto the busy waterfront, Fort Cochin to the west and Ernakulam on the mainland far to the east. Again, dining out on the lawn under the stars at night was heavenly. The ferries in our two day stay took us round to visit the Mattancherry Palace, St Frances Church where Vasco de Gama was first buried, the Jewish synagogue (the oldest in the Commonwealth) and the Basilica of Santa Cruz for Sunday mass. In the evening we went over to the mainland to watch Kathakali dancing.

# Delhi

Our final flight took us on to the capital Delhi. It felt so different from the easy going south of India – more modern and ruthless, where, as we found out, taxis can take you for a ride in both senses of the phrase. From there we just had to make the four-hour journey to Agra where I took the inevitable photograph of Mary with the Taj Mahal in the background. It was certainly an enchanting place to see.

Our time in the Indian subcontinent was now at an end. Trouble over not being able to show my transistor that had been booked into my passport on our second entry into India, being in our main luggage now aboard our plane, nearly caused us to miss the flight. It was a last-minute irritation and worry over Indian officialdom. But the end result, the delay getting aboard, meant we had to be sat first class as all the seats otherwise had been taken. In the nose of the jumbo jet we had splendid views flying over the Saudi Arabian desert, seeing little oases in the hollows below. It was our final picture of our much-filled three-month stay in the Orient.

# Southwold Again

Back in England, life in my Southwold practice began all over again. I wasn't to realise I had only three years to go. In the autumn of 1987, the practice took on a new partner, Dr Bill Tom, principally to be my assistant. My thinking was that I could then ease off a bit, and have more time for my developing complementary practice. But although Doctor Bill Tom couldn't have been a nicer guy, having been used to caring for my patients all by myself, I found sharing a bit disturbing. There is something very special in that personal relationship in a single practice that gets lost more and more with the increasing amalgamation of practices so much encouraged now. It must also be similar for patients. But as it happened, after a year Dr Tom and his wife had yearnings to return to Devon and left to join a practice there.

## Resignation from the NHS

To my mind, General Practice had its halcyon days in the 60s, 70s and 80s. Around the mid-60s the government started to subsidise practice premises, their receptionists and nurses. This did really help to update tatty old surgeries still making do with perhaps unsuitable rooms in the doctor's own house. It enabled me to rent more suitable rooms in the High Street. The ability to afford a receptionist meant I could start an appointment system and have someone to cover the phone instead of my wife during the day.

At that time, an American on holiday in Southwold made sneering remarks about the National Health Service. He described it as socialised medicine. I said he couldn't be further from the truth and that we had no interference from the government. We practised as we thought best. The government paid us of course but after that left us alone. I could look after patients without fear of the cost to them or them thinking I was making unnecessary calls for money. I could then prescribe what I liked and send patients to consultants and hospitals wherever I liked. With this freedom and independence and feeling one was doing a professional duty to be proud of, all started to change with the government interference in 1989.

The college of General Practitioners formed in the 60s, although I didn't myself join, definitely helped to raise the level of general practice – and with it its morale – to a height in the next three decades never to be reached again since.

The first inkling of change for economy reasons for the ever-increasing NHS budget occurred earlier in the 80s. Certain restrictions on prescribing were made. Most were sensible – medications for mild complaints that the patient could afford. There was however one drug on that list – Distalgesic – much prescribed and liked by practitioners at that time for moderate pain, that many in the profession objected to being taken off. My partner Nigel Drane and myself went to Jim Prior to complain. He had by then moved to the Upper House, pushed upstairs by Maggie Thatcher. When I took the chance to resent the fact that girls could be prescribed the Pill for contraceptive reasons without a prescription fee while women prescribed the same pill for medical reasons had to pay – Jim retorted very bitterly, "Oh you're a Roman Catholic." I think his bitterness came from his family. His mother, a very staunch Anglican, completely ostracised her sister, Jim's aunt, when she became a Catholic. She had a son Dick known to me as Gilman when in the same House a little above me at Ampleforth. He stayed on to become a monk as Brother, then Father Aidan. His mother Mrs Gilman was living at Southwold when we first arrived, so for many years we saw Dick when he came to visit her. When we bought Ford House, Dick came to bless every room including the loos. Jim had no idea of his cousin's existence. Over the years I had to tell each of them the other's happenings. Father Aidan became a housemaster and later took the unusual step in our times of becoming a hermit. Mary and

I visited him several times at his hermitage when in older age he moved from the remoteness of the moors to an isolated cottage in the valley below Ampleforth. On cards to us he referred to himself as Aidan, Dick, the mole. A card arrived one morning before Christmas 2018 signed that way with a large picture of a mole bearing the banner Happy Christmas. The same morning I had a phone call from the Abbey to say Father Aidan had just died. Distalgesic, by the way, was reinstated. Now it seems it isn't used at all.

## Early 1990

In early 1990 the then minister of health, in fact the Conservative Kenneth Clarke, set out a special contract for all to follow in general practice. A meeting was arranged at the Patrick Stead to explain this to all the local GPs. A young woman (she seemed just a girl to us elderly practitioners) came from the Suffolk Family Practitioner Authorities at Ipswich to spell out the details. For me, after already being uneasy about what I had heard about the contract, this was the last straw. I decided there and then to resign from my practice in the NHS and sent my six months' notice to the local Health Authorities. At the same time, I voiced my protest in letters to Kenneth Clarke, our local MP and local papers.

The one to the East Anglian Daily Times went as follows:

> **GP to resign in protest at new contracts**
> *A Suffolk GP is to resign from the National Health Service*
> *in protest at the new personal contracts being imposed on*
> *family doctors.*
>
> *Dr Christopher Hopkins will give up his job at the High Street*
> *surgery in Southwold on August 1 – two and a half years before he*
> *originally planned to retire.*
>
> *In a letter to the Suffolk Family Practitioner Committee,*
> *Dr Hopkins says his "moment of truth" came at a meeting to*
> *inform GPs of their obligations under the new contract. He said*
> *his forebodings came to a head when details of the practice leaflets,*

*which doctors were obliged to bring out from April 1, were being explained.*

*"A mature practitioner asked if he could not, for reasons of cost, leave out the map on it. He was told definitely not, and so it was spelled out, one item after another, how in future we practitioners cannot run our practices as we see fit without fear of penalty."*

*Under the new contracts, GPs will have to carry out routine medicals. Dr Hopkins said he had tried doing such examinations on all his 45 to 65-year-old patients 20 years ago. "I soon found the strain was too much when I still had to find time to look after the sick."*

### Homebound elderly
*He said recent surveys had shown regular medicals produced as much anxiety among patients as reassurance.*

*"How much worse is the strain going to be under the new contract, as for instance, chasing with my practice nurse, my 246 over-75 Southwoldians off the golf course, bowling green or dog walks into their homes once a year, where we are obliged to examine them or I face a penalty."*

*He said he used to praise the NHS to foreign visitors, especially Americans, about its freedom from red tape. Dr Hopkins said GPs were told that although they might not like the new contract, they would have to learn to live with it. "I, for one, now propose to live without it. I feel sorry for my colleagues I leave behind," he said.*

*Dr Hopkins has sent a copy of the letter to Health Secretary Kenneth Clarke and Waveney MP David Porter.*

To the Lowestoft Journal I also added what I now intended to do:

*A Southwold GP is resigning from the National Health Service in protest against new doctors' contracts which he has described as 'monstrous'. Dr Christopher Hopkins will give up his job at the High Street surgery in Southwold on August 1 – two and a half years before he originally planned to retire.*

*A Southwold GP for 32 years, Dr Hopkins described the new contracts, which came into force on Sunday, as "badly thought out by boffins in Whitehall".*

*"As an independent, professional man I think the whole thing is monstrous," he said.*

### *"Destroyed"*

*I feel we've got no freedom now to practise in the way that is best for our patients. We will be so inundated with bureaucracy and seeing fit people that we won't have time to treat the sick.*

*"The doctor-patient relationship is being destroyed by the lack of time for consultation with people who have real problems," he added.*

*Dr Hopkins, 62, said he had previously had no intention of retiring before he was 65 but could not now face the prospects of working under the new contract.*

*He announced his resignation in a letter to the Suffolk Family Practitioner Committee, which he said was doing its best but would now have to act as master by monitoring everything doctors did.*

### *Alternative*

*But although he is resigning from the NHS, Dr Hopkins will not be giving up medicine completely.*

*He plans to practise acupuncture and hypnotherapy from his home, two forms of alternative medicine which he makes available to NHS patients at his surgery.*

*"I did not want to give up being a GP and I was furious at the thought of going but now I'm looking forward to it and excited at the prospect of practising alternative medicine," he said.*

The letter had the instant advertising effect of a couple coming from Lowestoft for acupuncture.

It really struck home what I had done when driving one morning into Southwold a Lowestoft Journal poster on the pavement outside the newsagent displayed "Doctor quits NHS in protest".

I had the six months to work until my final departure. It felt on the last day rather like the end of term, a certain excitement and with the prospect of continuing my complementary medicine that I enjoyed privately, without too much regret. On my penultimate day I had a phone call from Radio Norfolk while on my rounds at Blythburgh Hospital. They must have kept a good diary. Someone wanted to come to interview me in half an hour about my resignation. Instant panic. Would I make a fool of myself? A few moments of utilising my self-hypnosis on the couch of the examination room and I was feeling quite calm. The young fellow, perhaps a novice, who came with his recorder seemed quite nervous.

The interview went well. Relief, then he said it was just a rehearsal. The repeat again went all right. Listening to Radio Norfolk's 8 o'clock news next morning I was quite pleased with my fluency. Again, it had an advertising effect. A year later I was phoned from a lady in Norfolk to see if I was the doctor on that broadcast. She wanted help with hypnotherapy.

On my final day, the sun shone. It was a Wednesday, my usual half day. I arranged to have as my very last patient the mother and son who had been my very first all those 32 years before. Mrs Green was still living at Walberswick. Her son, who in the meantime had become an airline pilot, was also there. I also invited the Southwold Mayor Sue Allen. Together with my receptionists Sheila and Joan we celebrated with champagne.

That evening I gave a party in the garden of Ford House for all those who had helped me through the years. First was Peggy Westall with one of her daughters from Cley, Norfolk. The Westall children had of course given me my first interview in their drawing room. Sadly, Peter after becoming a vicar at Kirton, took his own life a few years later. He had always been one of highs and lows. Our first two helps Greta and Carole were there, as well as two practice managers Wendy and Kash, and the practice nurse. Nigel Drane represented the partners. More champagne and eats. I made a speech describing and thanking everyone in turn. I am sure I thanked Mary too, as well as all the family present. They could never be too far away in a practice. It was a beautiful and happy evening. It felt a great relief to be at last never on call at night and have all my weekends free.

# EPILOGUE

EPILOGUE

# General Practice in Crisis

General Practice is now in crisis more than ever. Despite turning out more doctors in medical schools there is an alarming shortage of doctors. Even pleasant country towns are finding it difficult to fill posts. Since my retirement in 1990 the morale of the profession has become lower and lower. What has caused all this? Quite clearly it is the many directives imposed on practices by the Health Authorities that began at the time of my resignation. This has made practitioners feel more like post office clerks, being told what to do, rather than individuals acting on their own with professional pride. The resultant bureaucratic requirements have caused hours of form filling every day, with "Big Brother" making sure every box is ticked. Stress in GPs is rising, despite not being on call out of hours, paramedics dealing with emergency calls and nursing staff taking on more routine duties. Pay appears to be a sore point now despite what seemed to be an enormous rise towards the end of the last century. It has gone backwards in the last ten years, which is never liked by anyone, and pension schemes have become less favourable, making many retire earlier, another cause of the doctor shortage.

Is this general dissatisfaction worth it from the patient's point of view? Has the health of the nation improved over the past 30 years as a result of these targets and directives? Whether it has or not, it has certainly produced many drawbacks. The morale of a doctor must be most important. With a gross shortage of doctors, causing delay in getting an appointment and lack of time for a proper consultation, both can have vital consequences.

The present-day doctors complain of being overloaded by hospitals and having to be responsible for care of patients previously dealt with at outpatients, such as commencing treatment of diabetes and the onward care of chronic diseases such as emphysema and heart failure. It was being as far away from hospitals in a country practice (so that patients didn't expect me to be just a staging post) that attracted me to Southwold – in other words, to be a proper doctor. But with a shortage of practitioners and large lists not giving time, the resultant feeling of overload is understandable.

Has the present GP a more distant relationship with the hospital consultants? In my time it was very close, resulting in a very happy harmony and camaraderie. A local surgeon phoned me up soon after my arrival to welcome me. He didn't do much, if any, private practice so had no ulterior motive. Consultants were prepared to be phoned up for advice at their homes.

A gynaecologist at Ipswich, Hujohn Ripman, made a point of saying he was at home for a phone call at 7.00pm every evening. He in fact took personal responsibility for the antenatal care of all doctors' wives in the county and was present at all the deliveries. In this way he saw both our James and William into the world. If you or your family needed any medical care, most consultants then would see you privately with no question of a fee. Perhaps this was easier when more consultations took place in their homes rather than a clinic. You could also do a quid pro quo by sending them private patients.

One freedom that was present in the earlier days of the NHS was the ability to refer patients anywhere in Britain. You could send a patient to Edinburgh if you liked a particular consultant there. It has since become more restricted to each area and much more difficult to arrange. One factor that has made the medical profession as a whole in recent years less at ease is the fear of litigation. A doctor is expected to be superhuman and no errors are allowed. As a result, the cost of medical defence cover has soared.

What can be done to make General Practice more attractive and restore the GP's morale? Can he or she not be trusted to do their best for their patients without constant directives and financial inducement on different aspects of their care? Targets can be a distraction and prevent the full appraisal and use of the holistic approach. The competitiveness of Thatcherism had its good side when lists were relatively small and remuneration solely for each patient kept you on your toes. It was certainly better for the patient this way. To restore the morale of the GP he or she must be able to feel more of an individual and with less control and directives from above once more act with the pride of his or her profession.

## Mental Health

The media is obsessed with mental health. Much is mentioned of the lack of care for both the young and adults and the long waiting time to see mental health workers let alone psychiatrists.

The medical profession's standard treatment for mental illness is drugs and Cognitive Behaviour Therapy (CBT). It doesn't have much time for talking therapy, and hypnotherapy is rarely if ever utilised at all. It is the Cinderella of the profession. The only hospital that I know to use it which it does in several departments, is in my own county – the West Suffolk Hospital.

I have mentioned how useful I found hypnotherapy for the many cases of anxiety and need for relaxation in General Practice. I would plead with my fellow retired GPs, some quite young, that you could fill a gap in mental aid and will find the practice most fulfilling in addition to time on the golf course.

Since my retirement 29 years ago, I have been able to help over 100 patients with anxiety, over 60 with panic attacks, over 60 with depression and over 100 phobias, not to mention over 200 smokers. But what has been of special interest to me is Post Traumatic Stress Disorder (PTSD). For this I have combined hypnotherapy with a relatively new therapy, only discovered by a therapist Francine Shapiro in 1988, namely Eye Movement Desensitising and Reprocessing (EMDR). To my mind this is the 5-star treatment for PTSD. Bringing this up at a conference on the subject at the Royal Society of Medicine a few years ago, I seemed to be the only one using this combination then. Some were using hypnotherapy on its own, others EMDR or other therapies, but none the first two together.

It has been especially rewarding to have patients sent to me from the Rape and Abuse Centre in Lowestoft, when it was functioning, and to see the change that can be made in this way in the life of a sufferer of rape or abuse. It can happen in just two to three sessions. This therapy can also be most effective for phobias that so often start with one traumatic episode. As an example, a businessman coming to me in his sixties was suffering from height phobia. A recent panic attack walking near a cliff edge made him feel he had had enough. EMDR for the origin in the whispering gallery of St Paul's Cathedral aged 19, plus hypnotherapy, did the trick. Walking on the edge of Dunwich cliffs was then no problem, as also going over bridges.

Realizing how effective this therapy could be, I tried to advertise the fact to my fellow East Anglian practitioners in 2008 with most frustrating results. From a leaflet sent to over 100 practices I had just one reply – a practice manager wanting help for her son.

Feeling sorry for our servicemen suffering from PTSD and not always getting help, I wrote to the headquarters of the East Anglian regiment at Bury St Edmunds just returned from Afghanistan offering my services free (as I did for anyone unable to afford it). A Major replied regretting nothing could be done except through proper channels. At that point, when I had the time and energy at my disposal, I felt very sad. There must have been many sufferers I could have helped who were not getting it.

All the same, now in my nineties I am very lucky to have the satisfaction of continuing, even in a smaller way at this time of life, to still be of use to my fellow human beings. I do strongly advocate my fellow practitioners to do the same.

## Finale

Living a long life and keeping a good memory looking back through the years I have much to be thankful for. A happy childhood is the basis so essential for forming one's psyche and character. I was lucky in this. Luck has so often been at my side.

So often everything has fallen into place at the right time whether it was my schooling, my marriage, my practice at Southwold or the house I have lived in for the past 48 years. But most of all Mary and I have been blessed with a happy family. We have much to be proud about. Our eldest Frances followed in her mother's footsteps. As Mary's uncle Owen Ruane said at our wedding reception, referring to naming one of his racehorses after her – Mary Mac– it hadn't proved much of a racer but made a good breeder. So it was with Frances; she has brought up a family of four mostly on her own splendidly. Our next in line Christina (better known as Tina), after producing a boy and a girl, had a very successful teaching career and is now much missed after recently retiring from many years as deputy head at the Abbey School, Woodbridge. James, our eldest boy, was a big worry to us at school, and on leaving, as to what he was going to do in life. But he had the determination and skill in the business world, something of which his father had none. However, it was my nose noting a patient smelling of fish that started him as an entrepreneur in the fish market. Then changing to the building industry, he has now become the most successful builder in East Anglia, putting up over 1,000 houses a year. Our youngest, William, followed in his father's profession, specialising as a psychiatrist with psychotherapy as his main line. He is the chief psychiatrist at the Medical Foundation in London, dealing with the victims of torture. But how I like describing him best is to say he is – just William.

They in their turn have produced thirteen grandchildren and now three great-grandchildren. It has made a large loving and supportive family. At a time of so many broken ones, we have much to be grateful for. A final tribute to Mary my lovely wife: she never once complained at having to be housebound on the phone especially in those early days. She has produced our four splendid children, and for me the joy of helping it to happen.